# How to Write P
# Essays for Religious Studies
# A level

*New Edition completely revised*

Peter Baron

Published by Active Education

www.peped.org

Second Edition, First published in 2016

ISBN-13: 978-1539746355
ISBN-10: 1539746356

Cartoons used with permission © Becky Dyer

All images © their respective owners

*Links, reviews, news and revision materials available on peped.org*

The Peped.org website allows students and teachers to explore Philosophy of Religion and Ethics through handouts, film clips, presentations, case studies, extracts, games and academic articles.

Pitched just right, and so much more than a text book, here is a place to engage with critical reflection whatever your level. Marked student essays are also posted.

# Acknowledgements

My thanks to Brian Poxon for help in writing (and co-authoring) earlier versions of this book, one or two paragraphs of which remain here, and to Andrew Capone whose expert marking is reflected in some of the examples I have used, with permission.

# Contents

# Practical Essay Examples

1. "Kantian ethics is the best approach to issues surrounding abortion". Discuss. (Page 22).

2. Critically assess agent-centred as opposed to law-centred theories of ethics as a guide to practical decision-making. (Page 28)

3. Assess which theory of utilitarianism gives the best account of moral decision-making. (Page 35).

4. Distinguish between absolute and relativist morality. (Page 38)

5. To what extent can God reveal himself through sacred writings? (Page 43).

6. Evaluate Paley's arguments from design in the light of Dawkins' criticisms. (Page 46)

7. "Moral statements are merely an expression of feeling". Discuss. (Page 60).

8. To what extent can it be believed that religious experiences are no more than illusions? (Page 77)

9. To what extent is ethical language meaningful? (Page 87)

10. "Critically assess the view that free will and determinism are compatible". (Page 93)

11. Evaluate Hume's claim that miracles are the least likely events. (Page 113).

# Foreword to The Second Edition

This book is written by an experienced Religious Studies teacher who has spent his whole academic life doing philosophy, first at Oxford University, then Durham and Newcastle, and then in the classroom with generations of highly stimulating students.

The book is unique in this sense, that throughout the book I use practical examples from students writing (usually) under exam conditions in an exam hall. There is nothing fake about the marks they are awarded. I have also extensively rewritten this book in the second edition and added several new chapters on assessment, evaluation and diagnosis.

What I have tried to do is to extract some key principles of essay-writing in a highly analytical style, in a subject that involves complex issues. Trite answers, unclear reasoning, over-generalisation have no place in philosophy essays.

As well as a contents index, there is an index of practical examples with the actual essay titles used.

I have tried to range fairly widely across the A2 Ethics and Philosophy of Religion syllabuses, and provided strong as well as weak examples. I have used the new Developments in Christian Thought paper (OCR 2016 specification) to show how to construct your own essay questions and maybe even anticipate a question the examiner will ask (see page 92).

Further examples can be found on the peped.org website which is continually updated.

This book is dedicated to our students over the years who have given us so much stimulating food for thought.

# Understanding the Purpose

In this book I will concentrate on two approaches to writing philosophy essays. By 'philosophy' I mean everything included in the Religious Studies A level syllabus descriptions of ethics, philosophy and developments in religious thought, at A2 level. AS level requires a slightly different skill, as I will explain.

Let's be clear: the part a/part b distinction that exists at AS level, where you explain in part a and evaluate in part b, is not very helpful for developing essay-writing skills, because it pulls apart two skills that should be placed together (analysis and evaluation). It encourages you to learn to do something which you then unlearn at A2. For this reason OCR board has abandoned the part a/b split in its 2016 specification. Here I only consider A2 questions and answers that form one complete essay.

The two approaches I develop here I will call:

- Thesis-interpretation-development-explanation approach (**TIDE**)

- The asking questions about the question approach (**AQUAQ**)

I will also suggest they need to be used in different contexts. The first approach, **TIDE**, should be used when you clearly understand the issues involved with a particular question.

The second approach **AQUAQ** should be used especially when you are unsure what the issues are involved in the question.

After all, not all questions are crystal clear – some can be taken different ways, and even some in the past have been taken by students to refer to 18 different sections of the syllabus (see an example on page 18 below). None of this really matters. The only thing that matters is that you answer the question in an evaluative and analytical form of writing – and this too, I will teach you in this book.

Let me say at the start that not all teachers agree with my approach. In fact some teachers say things about essay-writing which I think are plainly wrong. Here is a list of some of the things you may have heard.

### 1. *"Don't use 'I', the personal pronoun"*.

I think it is wrong to teach this because this is simply not true to how real philosophers argue. Real philosophy is about identifying, owning and then presenting a crystal clear argument about some quite complex ideas. To own the argument it is perfectly legitimate to use 'I'. Teachers who say it is wrong to do this maybe have never read articles by academic philosophers. Articles start with what is called an **ABSTRACT** and an abstract is a summary of the thesis of the article. The thesis is the essence of the argument expressed as a single statement (discussed more fully in the next chapter), for example, 'in this essay I will argue that free will is not compatible with determinism because determinism requires a certain mechanistic view of causation which excludes the possibility of an uncaused will'. I am not at this stage asking you to understand my argument. I am asking you to understand my **THESIS** – and I think you would agree, it is clear. Whether I successfully argue the case is a different matter which we will consider later.

### 2. *"Don't ask questions in your essay"*.

This too is plainly wrong. Indeed my second approach involves interrogating the question. Imagine we face an exam question:

"Conscience is the voice of God, Discuss." What is meant by conscience? How do different thinkers such as Newman, Butler, Aquinas define it? Is the 'voice of God' a written text or something in my head? How can I know if it's really God's voice? These and other questions come to mind. Even if you don't like the idea of writing questions in your answer, at least do the interrogating as you think through your thesis.

### 3. "Do a general introduction of the major issues".

This is very dangerous if you're trying to be a philosopher. So many students drop grades by answering a question such as 'Explain and evaluate rule utilitarianism' by beginning with: "Mill was influenced by Bentham who was a hedonistic act utilitarian, but both come form a broader tradition which began with Epicurus and was developed by writers such as Hume as part of the general Enlightenment project to advance human welfare". This may be interesting (often it's not at all), it may be correct, but it is a big mistake because you have said nothing about rule utilitarianism whatever. You have wasted time and given the impression that you are a 'throw everything at the question and hope' sort of candidate, destined to achieve no greater than a C grade.

As the book progresses we will look at specific examples and explain what is good and bad about them. You can always do the same with an unmarked essay, in groups, trying to identify the kind of mistakes which I will summarise at the end of this book, together with a list of good things to aim for.

Here is a summary of a general strategy or purpose which we can practise and adopt as away of ensuring an A grade.

# 1. Attack the question

Questions contain ambiguous words, but they cannot contain any technical words not in the specification. A word like 'faith' which might appear in a question on the new Developments in Christian Thought OCR paper, is in fact highly ambiguous. It can mean "belief about" as in "I believe in the credal statements of the Church". It can mean 'optimism about the future' as in 'I have faith he will turn up tomorrow". And it can mean 'trust' as in "I have faith in Jesus Christ - he will get me through this mess".

Such ambiguity is found in the definitions of faith themselves, so we need to be careful not just to state a definition and leave it there (hanging in the air), but to discuss it fully. Just because someone learned has come up with a definition, doesn't mean the definition isn't itself in need of explanation and evaluation - it may be a very one-sided or deficient definition which you don't want to integrate into your argument. So leave it out, or integrate it properly.

For example, consider the Bible's own definition of faith found in the book of Hebrews (the author is unknown).

> *"Faith is confidence in what we hope for and assurance about what we do not see." Hebrews 11.1*

This definition is future-orientated - it speaks of faith which is directed towards future events. In this sense it cannot be talking about faith in historical events such as the life of Jesus. It must be speaking **ESCHATOLOGICALLY** perhaps about events at the end times (eschaton) when Christians believe the world will be wound up in one great second coming of Christ and a judgement. In Matthew's gospel we read of how at the end of time the 'sheep will be separated from the goats' according to how we have treated 'the least of all these" (Matthew 25).

Then the writer goes on to speak of 'things we do not see' such as the presence of God and the work of the Holy Spirit. God is invisible. He is also, many have faith to believe, immortal, omnipotent, holy, and magnificent. Perhaps the writer is referring to Christian belief in the great mystery of the Godhead, Father, Son and Holy Spirit, and their characteristics.

But (to make an evaluative point) what is missing from the definition in Hebrews? It says nothing about historical facts (which also may need faith to believe) such as the supposed 'fact' of the resurrection of Jesus. It says nothing, moreover, about personal relationship. Perhaps personal relationship is the key because it involves trust. Christians believe in a person who is present by the spirit and with whom it is meaningful to say 'I have a relationship with Christ". Now we are moving faith onto different territory - it is up to us in writing the essay to say which territory we wish to march across in our answer.

## 2. Answer the question

It sounds almost ridiculous when we say this: the greatest mistake students make every year at A level is not to answer the question in front of them. Instead, they answer a different question, and a model answer they have in their head is then supplied which occasionally they try to twist round to this question. Let me say now: this is a disastrous tactic if you want to get an A grade.

The corollary of this is that the same question can be asked in lots of different ways and we need to learn to spot them. For example, imagine we have a question on meta-ethics (that is, on the meaning of moral language) which says:

*"Moral language is just the expression of feelings". Discuss.*

This was the view of the emotivist philosopher AJ Ayer. But we can ask the same question a number of different ways.

*"Emotivism is a valid theory of ethical language". Discuss*

Or even what appears to be the opposite statement could be seen to be a reworking of this same answer:

*"Moral language is based on facts, not feelings", Discuss.*

This brings me to my third purpose in launching the essay.

# 3. Discuss the question even if it doesn't have the word 'discuss' in it

Later we will introduce and consider the place of 'trigger words' which are words which define what the examiner is asking you to do. "Discuss' is itself a trigger word. But what about this trigger, the phrase 'to what extent'?

**"TO WHAT EXTENT** is the ontological argument a valid argument for God's existence?"

The meaning of the 'to what extent' itself needs to be discussed. The question is asking whether there is validity in the ontological argument in its assumptions (some times called its preconditions), which include the view that the definition of God is ;'that which no greater thing can be conceived". Is this a 'good' definition of God and a valid starting point? Is it reasonable to have **A PRIORI** starting points for God's existence, or is God always going to be an argument about experience and fact - how things are and what we find by experience of actually living? The a priori is essentially an abstraction, meaning 'before experience'. But is the abstraction itself valid?

Then there is the question of how the ontological argument proceeds. It is essentially what is called a syllogism or logical relation between a number of statements.

a. God is greater than anything that can be conceived.

b. Because non-existence is an imperfection of being  - a more perfect idea of being exists which must include existence.

c. Therefore God, who has no imperfections, must exist.

As Gaunilo pointed out at the time, I can imagine a perfect island - an island greater than which cannot be conceived, but this doesn't imply the island actually exists. There is a false leap of logic included in the argument.

So our argument might be: "the ontological argument is invalid both in its preconditions, its process of reasoning, and in its conclusion. It is valid in no sense of the three implied meanings of the word 'valid' and so, to conclude, it is valid to no extent".

# 4. Take the question as you want to take it

In June 2015 the following question was asked in the OCR exam.

*"Evaluate the claim that moral judgements are based on an unquestionable intuitive knowledge of what is good". (OCR, 2015)*

Candidates split 50/50 as to whether this was a meta-ethics question (on the meaning of the word 'good') or whether it was a question about the meaning and role of conscience - as one definition of conscience, Aquinas' **SYNDERESIS**, means just this - an intuitive knowledge and inclination towards the good as an innate, shared state of human being.

Teachers rang me up describing how students had came out of the exam in tears because they believed the other interpretation of the question to the one they took was correct. But if they understood philosophy properly they would have grasped that any interpretation is valid depending how you argue your case. So have the courage to take the question as you want to take it.

Just to underline this point: this is what the examiner wrote in the mark scheme on this question:

*Either a meta-ethical or a conscience approach to this question could be credited. Candidates could also use a combination of meta-ethics and conscience to answer this question.*

*Alternatively, some candidates may make the link that 'good' is known through practical decision making. They may include utilitarian concepts of hedonic naturalism where good is known by what gives pleasure, or might suggest a virtue ethics approach as a way of*

*overcoming Moore's mysterious 'good' and the naturalistic fallacy*
*with the point that there is not a fact/value problem with this*
*approach and that Moore was part of the problem described by*
*Anscombe.*

*Candidates may wish to define what they mean by 'moral*
*judgements' (OCR Mark Scheme, G582 Q2, June 2015)*

I think the examiner here is referring to Anscombe's 1956 essay which argues that moral philosophy has argued itself into a dead end and lost its way with the obsession with the meaning of the word 'good', and the neglect of the role of character in ethics. I'm not sure if any candidates followed the third route suggested by the examiner - which would have taken some nerve, in arguing that 'goodness' emerges through practical decision-making by an experiential route.

# Constructing the Thesis

Philosophy essays (Moral Philosophy, Philosophical Theology or Philosophy of Religion) are essays of a certain sort unique to this subject. This is because they involve construction and evaluation of arguments, and because their style is characterised by great clarity and relevance. In this chapter we consider the first of two approaches to writing essays, what we can call the **TIDE** approach (thesis-interpretation-development-explanation).

An argument is not an opinion. An opinion says "I prefer tea to coffee", or "I think Mill's view of utilitarianism is superior to Bentham's". Whereas an argument justifies this **ASSERTION** by careful consideration of different positions - "Mill's rule utilitarianism presents a case for justice and minority rights based on a general sympathy which elevates it above the hedonism of Bentham".

Also, an argument is not a feeling. Arguments proceed by reasoning, and so there is such a thing as a false move or **FALLACY** in an argument. It is the nature of sound arguments that the conclusion must follow from what you have said, after carefully weighing **ALTERNATIVE VIEWPOINTS**.

Above all, philosophy essays are characterised by **LOGICAL ANALYSIS**. In the sections that follow we explore and then apply principles of how to write logically and analytically.

# Constructing an argument

## The Thesis

A philosophy essay has a main point or **THESIS**. A thesis is one sentence which sums up what you are trying to establish as your conclusion.

When you are faced with an essay title, practise constructing your thesis in one sentence. This thesis will then appear in your introduction (see below for how this can thesis statement can be introduced).

## Practical Example 1

> *"Kantian ethics is the best approach to issues surrounding euthanasia", Discuss.*

Thesis: Kantian ethics is incapable of considering the complexities of individual ethical dilemmas at the end of life, as it is based on absolutes derived from the categorical imperative.

This thesis is clear, brief, and relevant to the question set. I am not trying to prove the thesis here, that will form the substance of my essay, but I am stating it so the reader is completely clear as to what that thesis is.

## The argument

My conclusion about Kantian ethics needs to follow from the argument that I have constructed. One way of making sure this happens is to put the thesis as the conclusion of a set of **PREMISES** or starting points - assertions I am prepared to justify in my essay as the paragraphs unfold. In my simple example below I have two premises.

- **PREMISE 1** - Kantian ethics is the ethics of universal duties established by universalising your behaviour by an a priori method.

- **PREMISE 2** - An a priori method cannot consider individual circumstances as it is a form of abstract, generalised reasoning using the imagination.

- **CONCLUSION** - Therefore Kantian ethics is unable to treat euthanasia on a case by case basis necessary to be of use to the individual facing moral dilemmas.

Another example of an argument that moves from premises to conclusion is the **ONTOLOGICAL ARGUMENT** for the existence of God mentioned earlier. This argument is an a priori deductive argument (meaning one that moves from premises to conclusion by logic rather than appeal to facts).

- **PREMISE 1** - God is a being greater than which no being can be conceived.

- **PREMISE 2** - Even the atheist has an idea of God in his head.

- **PREMISE 3** - It is greater for something to exist in reality and the mind than it is to exist in the mind alone.

- **PREMISE 4** - If God exists in the mind alone, this contradicts our definition of God, because it would be possible for something greater than God to exist.

23

- **CONCLUSION** - Therefore a being called God must exist.

One possible structure for an essay on the ontological argument is to examine and then evaluate these premises one by one.

For example, look at premise 1, that God is a being greater than which no being can be conceived (also considered in chapter 1). If we consider the Christian view of God, then it could be argued that God has moral flaws: he is angry, jealous of rivals, judges people and sentences some to hell. In this case we can argue the premise is false as we can conceive of a greater God.

In addition, the argument is often criticised as committing a **BARE ASSERTION FALLACY**, as it offers no supportive premise other than qualities inherent in the unproven statement of premise 1. This is also called a circular argument, because the premise relies on the conclusion, which in turn relies on the premise. Whatever statements (premises) you can think of to support a conclusion (thesis), the paragraph structure can explore the outline argument structure stage by stage, ensuring logic and clarity.

# Worldview

Sometimes, it is necessary to examine the worldview of an author to make the premises explicit or to find the missing premise. The worldview is often governed by culturally specific assumptions the author makes. Taking our major ethical theories as an example, here is a summary of the major worldviews and the assumptions they make. If you disagree with the assumption, and can establish it as questionable or even false, you destroy the argument. The table opposite identifies some features of the worldview underlying major ethical theories.

| THEORY | ASSUMPTIONS | OBJECTIONS |
| --- | --- | --- |
| Relativism | There is no universal truth. | May be empirically false |
| Natural law | Humans by nature do good | Humans by nature are selfish and do more evil than good |
| Kantian ethics | Reason is divided between the noumenal and phenomenal realms, and morality belongs to the noumenal. | Moral principles seem to be derived by many philosophers from the natural or empirical world eg by adding up happiness. |
| Utilitarianism - Bentham | Pleasure is the only good. We can measure pleasure. | There seem to be other "goods" such as duty. We can't measure pleasure in hedons or anything else. |
| Divine Command | God's word is clear and unambiguous on practical issues. | Ancient texts were written from one cultural perspective which often does not address our culture directly. |

| Utilitarianism - Mill | There are higher and lower pleasures | This is a difficult distinction to make without sounding snobbish. |
|---|---|---|
| | Rules are needed to maximise utility | |
| | | Rules imply universal application - so when can you break them? |
| Virtue ethics | A virtue is an agreed character trait. This trait comes from the rational purpose (telos) of human beings. | We cannot agree on whether things like courage are really a moral virtue. What about the kamikaze pilot? |

The above table can be added to. The idea is to expose the assumptions within the premises of an argument, as the easiest way to expose an argument as false is to expose the premise as false - or based on a faulty assumption. An assumption is not an argument but a starting-point.

# Creating sequences of thought

An argument proceeds by a sequence of thought where one idea follows clearly from another. This means it is essential you construct an outline before you start to write. One way of ensuring the argument is sequential (rather than a jumbled up series of loosely related points) is to use link phrases. Here is a list.

- I will begin by
- The argument of this essay is that
- Here we need to consider the following objection
- In the next paragraph, I consider
- Having argued that X, I now wish to consider Y
- Although I have shown X, I still need to establish Y
- Some might object that
- Further support for this claim comes from W's argument.

Notice that a number of these use the personal pronoun "I". We considered why this was perfectly valid in our opening chapter. The use of 'I' is deliberate, as a philosophy essay is my own analysis of a question. I need to form a clear conclusion - which is my own view, fully justified, and therefore the use of "I" (unlike in other subjects) is to be encouraged.

If you want to use analytical words, here's another list. Some of these are **DEVELOPING** the argument in one line or direction, and others are **CONTRASTING** another argument with your previous line of argument:

- However
- Because (insert name of philosopher) argues this………..
- It could be argued therefore
- With regard to this
- On the other hand
- It follows from this

- It can thus be seen that

- Alternatively

- Moreover

- Furthermore

- In addition to this

- Subsequently

- Consequently

- As a result

- This would suggest

- Such an argument leads

- Kant's (or another philosopher) argument might work if….., however,

- Aquinas (or another philosopher) is wrong however, because (we can say a philosopher is wrong, but need to say why and show how).

## Practical Example 2

**Critically assess agent-centred as opposed to law-centred theories of ethics as a guide to practical decision-making.**

*Within the philosophy of ethics, agent-centred theories of ethics are those, such as Virtue Ethics, which encourage the development of moral characters rather than universal commands as in law-centred theories of ethics such as in Kantian Ethics and focus on the promotion of virtues, (Greek: arete) such as faith, hope and charity in order to develop practical wisdom (phronesis) rather than strict criteria for action such as the Hedonic Calculus in Utilitarianism. Thus, although law-centred ethical theories such as Kantian Ethics and Utilitarianism can enable the construction of universal laws, such as the Universal Declaration of Human Rights, this essay will argue that agent-centred theories of ethics, such as Virtue Ethics, are an ethically superior guide to practical decision-making as they can overcome cultural differences, promote spontaneous but principled acts of virtue, and lead to the development of moral characters through the processes of emulation, education and experience, leading to practical moral wisdom.*

Notice the very clear thesis statement in the final sentence. The essay also launches with a very clear contrast with law-based ethics of, for example Kant. The candidate is quite rightly comfortable using the personal pronoun 'I'.

*Firstly, whereas law-based theories of ethics revolve around the propagation of absolute, universal laws which are true for all time and all places, agent-centred theories of ethics are much more relativistic and as such are superior as a guide to practical-decision making as they take into account the different values, beliefs and customs that different cultures and societies throughout the world adhere to. For example, whereas in China there is still a single baby policy and so sexual intercourse after the birth of the first child is condemned, in more liberal societies such as Britain, the use of contraception are more tolerated as sexual intercourse can lead to the development of intimate and personal virtues such as trust, compassion and love. Indeed, the Ancient Greek Philosopher, Aristotle would claim that these virtues can lead to the development of practical wisdom when making decisions surrounding sexual ethics as rather than leading to* self-deprivation which is the deficiency, or over-dependence which is the excess, they can lead to love, which is the Golden Mean.

An interesting theme is developing here - that virtue ethics is superior because it is relativistic. Practical wisdom or phronesis is used to illustrate the importance of judgement in sexual ethics.

*Likewise, within religion, it can be claimed that agent-centred theories of ethics are superior as rather than upholding universal and absolute truths as in Roman Catholicism, such as the prohibition of abortion, agent-centred theories can adopt a teleological approach and consider what is in the best interests of those parties involved and retain the flexibility to decide when abortion may be the best course of action to take when confronted with a scenario involving a pregnant teenage rape victim, for example. Consequently, although law-based theories of ethics can enable the establishment of universal laws, it must be argued that as morality is a relativistic feature of the world and varies between different cultures and societies, that as agent-centred theories best accommodate for these differences, they must be argued to be the more superior type of ethical theory when it comes to practical decision making.*

The teleological nature of virtue ethics is considered - the candidate might have alluded to the ultimate telos of the flourishing life lived within the flourishing society (eudaimonia)

*Additionally, although law-based theories of ethics can enable the establishment of a common-ground of morality between different individuals, social groups, and society through the promotion of universal laws such as King John's Magna Carta, which is often used in courts around the world, that they promote the passive acceptance of moral guidance rather than the active involvement in times of practical-decision making as in agent-centred theories of ethics, agent-centred theories must be argued to be the most helpful.*

*Indeed, the modern virtue ethicist, Alasdair McIntyre has claimed that due to the predominance of law-based theories of ethics in the age of modernity through the forms of Utilitarianism's Hedonic Calculus or Kant's categorical imperatives, modern society has produced three archetypal characters; the bureaucratic and ruthless manager who takes no account of virtues and moral principles when making decisions relating to business ethics, the rich aesthete whose primary concern is immediate gratification that they forget to take time to reflect on their actions and develop moral wisdom, and the therapist who is responsible for clearing up the mess that the two former characters create. Thus, he claims that the flaw in law-based theories of ethics is that rather than encouraging virtuous moral agents, they promote the usefulness of law-based theories of ethics to the extent that society is docile in its acceptance of moral laws and commandments that it takes no account of how those laws fit in with the society that it faces. For example, whereas the Marriage (Same Sex Couples) Act did not become legislation until 2013, the equality movement begun a considerable amount of time before that. Therefore, not only does law-centred theories of ethics deny the involvement of individuals in creating a sense of morality that is relevant to their time, they are so bound by laws that they can become invalidated as society progresses and most therefore be argued to be an inferior ethical guide to practical decision-making.*

Some excellent evaluative points giving the strengths of virtue ethics are here illustrated by Alasdair MacIntyre's three archetypes, the bureaucrat , the aesthete and the therapist. All three avoid moral thinking and therefore promote amoral or even immoral behaviour.

*Finally, as a result of agent-centred theories of ethics' encouragement of individuals' activity in the development of morality, they can also lead to the development of moral characters which set an example for what society ought to become and as such must be argued to be ethically superior guides to ethical decision-making. Indeed, at the centre of Aristotle's philosophical project was the development from potentiality, that is, what a person could become, to actuality, that is, what a person ought to become through the processes of emulation, education, and experience which lead to the development of practical wisdom, or phronesis, and therefore moral perfection, or eudaimonia.*

At last the candidate mentions eudaimonia, which might have been introduced earlier as the ultimate telos or goal of virtue ethics. Again excellent use of a philosopher's (Aristotle) argument from potentiality.

*Subsequently, it can be argued that through the process of emulation, agent-centred theories of ethics are superior to law-centred theories of ethics as rather than encouraging individuals to align their actions with pre-set moral laws and commands, they encourage individuals to base their actions on moral role models such as Martin Luther King, Elizabeth Fry and Ghandi which they discover through the process of education and exploration and which they become more like through their moral experiences and attempts at practical decision-making. Thus, although agent-centred theories of ethics can be criticised when it comes to practical decision-making for taking no account of post-modern societies' divergence away from moralistic beliefs due to the process of individualisation and as such our role models have become*

*McIntyre's rich aesthetes, this can be overcome by the claim that individuals are aspiring to people who lack the Golden Mean of Virtue Ethics and who possess too many excesses in terms of boastfulness, celebrity status and magnificence rather the true role models who are those who are the hardest to find and can only be found through moral experience and exploration as in Plato's Cave.*

Stylistically the sentences are becoming a little too long and breathless, but the points are still being well made. Note how this candidate keeps the main thesis to the forefront, which is excellent technique. Also allusions to Plato's Cave show ability to cross syllabus areas and show what is called 'synoptic understanding'. Strong candidates show a sort of courage in their writing, making associations and linkages freely and in a way that sets the essay apart.

*In conclusion, although agent-centred theories of ethics can be criticised for their inability to set universal laws which create a unified version of ethics and which can therefore be readily applied, that agent-centred theories of ethics can overcome the barriers that law-centred theories of ethics are associated with, such as the cultural and religious relativity of morality as society has progressed in recent years and stimulate the promotion of spontaneous moral acts through the development of moral characters through the processes of emulation, education, and experience, they must be upheld as the most practical theories of ethics when it comes to ethical decision making as they promote respect, love and compassion rather than the inflexibility and passivity that law-centred ethical theories have historically caused in overcoming social inequality and developing virtuous role models.*

The main point of the essay is summed up and rounded off. An excellent attempt, gaining close to full marks at A2 level. The criteria of assessment are discussed in a later chapter - you can return to this essay and see how the levels of criteria and the focus of the assessment is made according to ability to address the question, knowledge and understanding, relevance, use of scholars, and analytical and evaluative writing.

# Introduction and Conclusion

Philosophical essay writing argues for a **THESIS** (a basic position on an issue) and needs to state this thesis in the introductory paragraph. Sometimes we may be unsure of what line to take on an essay title. If we are unsure we need to adopt a different approach - to ask questions about the question. I call this, the second of my two approaches, the **AQUAQ** approach.

To illustrate how this works, let's take an essay title such as "Assess which theory of utilitarianism gives the best account of moral decision-making".

## Practical Example 3

**"Assess which theory of utilitarianism gives the best account of moral decision-making".**

Here are three questions (of many) we might ask about this question.

1. How does utilitarianism arrive at a meaning of the good?

2. Which of the three utilitarian theories presents the most practical account when the meaning is applied to a situation?

3. What do we mean by "best" in the sense of moral decision-making?

We then have a tailor-made paragraph structure.

- **PARAGRAPH 1** - Utilitarianism arrives at goodness by assuming one intrinsic good, happiness or pleasure, and then arguing for an empirical calculation of the balance of pleasure or happiness over pain. It is a scientific approach which has the benefit that everyone is treated as equal, and the thing maximised is supposedly easy to calculate.

- **PARAGRAPHS 2 AND 3** - Bentham's account is hedonic as it is based on the idea of measuring pleasure in hedons. This is difficult to do in practice as there is no clear indication that my hedon value equals yours - for instance, I award a Mars bar three hedons and you award it four. Also the idea of maximising utility doesn't account of the problem of average utility, as an average may rise when one person is given a huge increase in pleasure. There is generally a problem of distribution o utilitarian ethics. Mill tried to escape this problem by arguing for justice in distribution of benefits and equal rights. But his compromise may not work because he himself allows us to break a rule if there is a clear utilitarian case.

- **PARAGRAPH 4** - In contrast, Peter Singer's utilitarian ethic rests on the maximising of first choices. This is a simple vote on a stated preference, we are not asked to weigh hedons and add them up. The student could explain how this works and then come to a decision as to which is superior as an approach. But the conclusion here unfolds as part of the analysis.

An alternative suggested earlier is that we work out our thesis in advance and then state it straightaway in the introductory paragraph. The thesis is then restated at the end, with additions and qualifications judged relevant from the whole essay. The thesis doesn't have to be the very first sentence, but here I will make it the first sentence.

> *"I will argue that Mill's utilitarianism, with its emphasis on social rules and higher and lower pleasures, is superior to Bentham's act utilitarianism and Singer's preference utilitarianism as it protects individual rights and places justice as the prime concern of utilitarian ethics. By contrast, Singer places too much emphasis on rational choice, thereby devaluing the sanctity of life of the unborn and the new born up to eight weeks old. Bentham, in addition, places over-reliance on an empirical measurement of pleasure and wrongly argues that pleasure is the supreme good".*

This is the position I am seeking to defend which will be worked out in the bulk of the essay. Notice that no examiner can accuse me of not answering the question, and as long as I keep disciplined in my thought process, I simply amplify the thesis stated at the beginning of my essay and restate it as a conclusion. I could equally well have preferred Bentham's utilitarianism or Singer's: I would have marshalled my argument a different way but the technique of producing an argument justified and illustrated appropriately remains identical.

# Practical Example 4: strong and weak introductions and conclusions

## "Distinguish between absolute and relative morality".

*"With ethics, morality can be either absolute or relative. It cannot be both, however, many religious ethics may have part of their ethics as relative and part as absolute."*

This is a weak opening for two reasons. First, it doesn't say anything substantial. Why not define the two terms or present a contrast between them? Secondly, it manages to contradict itself. The essay says first, that theories cannot contain elements of both and then, that theories do contain elements of both. In an actual OCR AS exam this essay scored 13/25.

Notice again that in AS questions we are only asked to do a part of an essay. Part a) answers should take thirty minutes, and are descriptive in nature rather than evaluative. To reiterate: OCR have ditched the distinction from 2016, other exam boards haven't.

Hence it is important to launch straight into your answer without too much introductory material. So, as mentioned when we considered the essay on Irenaeus earlier, it's often best to begin with a definition of the key terms - in this case the words "absolute" and "relative", and your thesis could be to explain the ambiguities in each term (for example, absolute can mean *universal*, or *having no exceptions*, or *objective*), and then apply them to a specific example.

**"Explain the concept of relativist morality". (OCR June 2009).**

*"A moral relativist would question "what do we mean by good?" when deliberating the best, most moral action to take when faced with an ethical decision. An example of a relativist moral statement is, "I ought not to steal because I will cause suffering to those I steal from." This is a reasonable statement, considering the consequences of a potential action. It is teleological, in that it is concerned with ends (Greek word "telos" meaning end or purpose). Relativism is in direct contrast with absolute morality which is deontological and concerned with the actions themselves. A moral relativist would not believe that there is a fixed set of moral rules that apply to all people all times, in all places. Rather, they would leave the morality is changeable and differs culture to culture time to time, and place to place. This idea is known as cultural relativism."*

This paragraph successfully launches the answer by making a clear distinction between absolute and relative morality, defining the terms, and going straight to the heart of the difference between the two concepts. Although the word 'absolute' is not contained in the title, it is always a good tactic to set up a contrast between two ideas, such that the differences between them highlight the essential nature of relativism. The key contrast is set up with the link word "rather". The essay scored 25/25.

# Command Words

**COMMAND WORDS OR TRIGGER WORDS** - are words in the title which require a certain line of analysis or evaluation. What is the difference between the two concepts?

**ANALYSIS** - provides the reasons that establish a conclusion. In other words, the analysis supports the conclusion.

Imagine I am given a car to test. On one level I can analyse how it works. I can look at the engine design and the number of seats, the aerodynamics. I can explain the linkages between wheels and engine, the power to weight ratio, the acceleration.

Then, I can move on to **EVALUATE** the car. I can do this in two ways.

1. I can compare the car with another to see which is **BETTER**. So I can do the same in Philosophy, by comparing Kantian ethics with Utilitarian ethics, for example - which gives the better account of morality (of course, "better' here needs definition). Do I mean, more easy to apply, more understandable, or more realistic in light of human psychology?). If we are not being asked to evaluate, then we shouldn't really be presenting such a contrast.

2. I can evaluate the car against some **OBJECTIVE** standard. For example, there may be objective measures of how a car handles, such as the famous Elk test in Sweden by which a car is braked very hard on an icy road to see if it turns over. One famous make of car did turn over, to the embarrassment of the manufacturer! We may do the same in Philosophy. There are objective tests for the logic of arguments - as the chapter on fallacies explains.

Here, then are the main command words (words in the title).

- **ACCOUNT FOR** - requires an answer that gives the reasons for the subject of the question.

- **ANALYSE** - requires an answer that takes apart an idea, concept or statement in order to consider all the factors it consists of. Answers of this type should be very methodical and logically organised.

- **ASSESS** - requires a weighing of an argument to consider its main features, and the strengths and weaknesses of elements of the argument.

- **COMPARE** - requires an answer that sets items side by side and shows their similarities and differences. A balanced (fair, objective) answer is expected.

- **CONSIDER** - requires an answer in which the students describe and give their thoughts on the subject.

- **CONTRAST** - requires an answer that points out only the differences between two ideas or theories.

- **CRITICISE** - requires an answer that points out mistakes or weaknesses, and that also indicates any favourable aspects of the subject of the question. It requires a balanced answer.

- **CRITICALLY COMPARE** - newly adopted by the OCR board in 2016, this implies placing two sets of ideas alongside each other and pointing out their similarities and differences, whilst also evaluating the good and bad things about each.

- **DEFINE** - requires an answer that explains the precise meaning of a concept.

- **DESCRIBE** - requires an answer that says what something is like, how it works and what is essential features are.

- **DISCUSS** - requires an answer that explains an idea or concept, and then gives details about it with supportive information, examples, points for and against, and explanations for the facts put forward. It is important to give both sides of an argument and come to a conclusion.

- **ELUCIDATE** - requires an answer that explains what something means, makes it clear (lucid).

- **EVALUATE** - require an answer that decides and explains how great, valuable or important something is. The judgement should be backed by a discussion of the evidence or reasoning involved.

- **EXPLAIN** - requires an answer that offers a rather detailed and exact explanation of an idea or principle, or a set of reasons for a situation or attitude.

- **EXPLORE** - requires an answer that examines the subject thoroughly and considers it from a variety of viewpoints.

- **ILLUSTRATE** - requires an answer that consists mainly of examples to demonstrate or prove the subject of the question. It is often added to another instruction.

- **JUSTIFY** - requires an answer that gives only the reasons for a position or argument. Answer the main objections likely to be made of them. Note, however, that the proposition to be argued may be a negative one (e.g. Justify the abolition of the death penalty.)

- **STATE** - requires an answer that expresses the relevant points briefly and clearly without lengthy discussion or minor details.

- **SUMMARISE/OUTLINE** - require an answer that contains a summary of all the available information about a subject, i.e. only the main points and not the details should be included. Questions of this type often require short answers.

- **TRACE** - is found most frequently in historical questions (but not only in History courses); it requires the statement and brief description in logical or chronological order of the stages (steps) in the development of e.g. a theory, a person's life, a process, etc.

- **TO WHAT EXTENT IS X TRUE?** - requires an answer that discusses and explains in what ways X is true and in what ways X is not true.

# Practical Example 5

In this example we analyse how the phrase "to what extent" in the list of **COMMAND WORDS** might be developed. Again, our comments are in italics.

## To what extent can God reveal himself through sacred writings? (OCR, January 2012)

*"There are two broad categories under which the interpretation of religious writings comes; the propositional view of revelation*

*and the non-propositional. The propositional view holds that sacred writings are a direct revelation from the creator, or from a divine force; they are written precisely as intended, not a jot of their content may be questioned or changed. This is the traditional view of Christianity, Judaism and Islam. Under the propositional view, the sacred text is explicitly stating propositions which are taken by the believer to be absolute truth".*

The student here opts not to launch with a thesis or argument that is clearly stated, but rather with a description of the propositional view. The description isn't very strong: it is highly disputable that Christianity takes the same view as Islam about sacred writings - Islam believes the Qur'an is dictated by the Angel Gabriel, whereas Christianity has adopted different approaches to interpreting Scripture, and in the Middle Ages, the allegorical method was highly popular whereby the Song of Songs became an allegory for Christ and his beloved church (for example).

# Conclusions

Using the same two essays on relativism in example 5, we can clearly see the difference between a strong and weak conclusion.

## Essay 1

*"In conclusion, both relative and absolute morality have many pros and cons. Neither one is better than the other , because they are extremely different."*

What is wrong with this conclusion? First of all, the student was asked to distinguish between absolute and relative morality, not evaluate the two (which means compare and say which is stronger or weaker as a theory of ethics). Secondly, the student doesn't present a clear, reasoned opinion. To say "there are pros and cons for each theory" doesn't tell us what they are, nor does it suggest any implications - even if this point were relevant (which it isn't as it is evaluating not distinguishing). The analysis here should have been by way of **CONTRAST** between the two, and the conclusion should have reworked the contrast.

## Essay 2

*"An example of changing morality between cultures is infanticide which was practised by the Greeks and Romans. Everyone in our modern society considers this completely wrong and immoral. However, for them, there was no problem with it. It was socially accepted. Similarly, in Islamic cultures, many of the women choose to wear head scarves as a mark of their faith. Many people in all other cultures see this to be unfair and restricting, a way of taking away the woman's rights to be individual. However the woman make the choice to do it because in their culture and their mind, it is considered morally acceptable and common practice. Advocates of moral relativism see the diverse nature of our world and the existence of many different ethical viewpoints as proof that no moral absolutes exist. For moral relativist thinkers such as Protagoras, Aristotle and more recently Summer and Mackie, morality is relative to place, time and culture. They find examples within our world and differing societies to support the moral viewpoints".*

Above is the conclusion to the full mark answer "explain the concept of relative morality". The conclusion here is strong, and also qualified by words (underlined) such as "however" and "similarly" which are indicators of an attempt to analyse rather than just describe. Notice also the use of examples, and the introduction of authors' names. It is also fully relevant to the question, not deviating into evaluation when it isn't asked for.

# Practical Example 6:

### Evaluate Paley's argument from design in the light of Dawkins' criticisms (OCR)

*Having analysed and evaluated several key elements of Paley's argument from design, and critically compared scholarly views, I would suggest that Dawkins' strongest counter-argument carries more philosophical weight. When Dawkins suggests that bees are unaware of the shape of the honeycomb, or flowers not cognisant of any Fibonacci code, but that these structures are simply most efficient for survival, then any element of a need for, or postulation of, a Designer, becomes redundant. DNA and its survival through genetic continuation wins the day; any superimposed element of pattern or design in nature is a man-made construct. Even if design is apparent in the things man makes, such as a watch, there is no sense in which this can be taken to mean blind nature has design and, by extension, a Designer. Thus I would argue, as I have done throughout, that 'the design argument is not a convincing proof for God.'*

This is a very strong, top-level conclusion because in the final sentence the student has quoted the question and drawn the analysis back towards the question. The thesis is clear and powerfully summed up; it is well illustrated; it has good illustration and mention of relevant scholars.

To repeat: the conclusion restates the main thesis in a slightly more nuanced (qualified) form and makes crystal clear what this answer to this question is.

# Mind-mapping the Grand Scheme

## Mind-maps

A mind map is a visual and logical representation of a complex set of relationships. It is statement of those relationships rather than an explanation, but it does provide us with a scaffolding on which to hang an argument.

Here is one example of a mindmap on the key ethical theory of Natural Law. It presents us with a way of arguing about this theories. You can use these and develop it for yourself and try producing your own for areas of the syllabus not discussed in this book. The technique would be the same.

1. Think through what is the starting point. Are there any assumptions the theory makes about the world or human nature.

2. Think through the end or final point of the theory. For example, Kant claims that a world of human beings obeying the categorical imperative will be the best of all possible worlds or summum bonum. What is the relationship between the three Kantian postulates (or **ASSUMPTIONS**) of autonomy (self-rule), immortality and God? Puzzling through this kind of relationship will help you construct a argument about Kant.

3. What are the key steps a philosopher takes to move from

assumption to conclusion? Again, using Kant as an example, it is the categorical imperative which really helps us define what is good and gives us the right motive for action - "duty for duty's sake".

So, in summary, a mind-map sketches out a skeletal structure and allows us to take a starting point in our analysis. It is a useful memory aid for an exam, and also ensures the essay moves in a logical direction. Philosophical views and theories can be mapped in different ways. Here is one way for the theory of Natural Law.

I take as my starting point the assumption of **SYNDERESIS** in Aquinas' theory, because he states that all human beings have an innate knowledge of first principles (the primary precepts). In general we are born with the desire to "do good and avoid evil". Slightly confusingly, Aquinas calls this the 'first principle of the natural law' not to be confused with 'primary precepts'. It might be seen as a starting point because according to Aquinas, we by our nature pursue good ends which are rational. These good ends are the primary precepts which lead to personal and social flourishing, So, if we didn't want to do good, we wouldn't want to pursue rational ends.

The primary precepts are then applied to produce secondary precepts. Notice the ones listed are Roman Catholic applications which may be disputed. No secondary precept is absolute, although when we read Catholic documents such as Veritatis Splendor (1995) the secondary principles seem to be presented as absolutes.

We now have a logical structure for any essay.

# Natural Law Mindmap

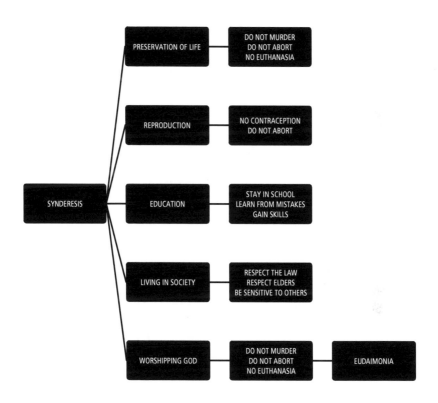

# Lego Blocks

We can use lego blocks to build up a scholar's argument where each block represents a key idea. This is just a visualisation of an argument. Those blocks could all be of one colour; however, there could be other blocks that are of a different colour which act as examples the scholar uses at various points throughout their arguments – where would you place those examples in the structure?

Other coloured blocks are the additional points the scholar makes, but you have decided that they are not strictly relevant to the question you are answering at this point. When you look at the tower, do you clearly know and understand what part of the argument the blocks represent? If you do, some potentially good analysis has gone on.

# Jenga Blocks

This exercise can also be done with Jenga blocks. This enables you to make a link between **ANALYSIS** (A follows from B) and **EVALUATION** (X is stronger than Y). The blocks can be built up bit by bit, with each block representing a part of a scholar's argument.

A person then has to evaluate the argument that you have built up, and remove a block – that block representing part of the argument the scholar has put forward. If you feel you want to defend that scholar then you can replace that block that has been removed by your interlocutor (a fancy word for the person who is questioning you), if you feel you can say how that scholar would respond to the person making the counter-argument.

You can try to attack an argument at its base, not at the end of the argument where it might have a few less secure sections. Maybe we all have parts of our arguments that are weaker at their fringes but we like to think our main principles are built on more solid ground. But imagine how devastating it would be to attack an argument at its base; the entire Jenga tower falls and the argument has to be built up again.

**If you want to attack an argument one effective way of doing so is to attack the base assumptions.**

For example, Brian Davies has raised the point that it does not take a God to guarantee Kant's summum bonum – maybe a pantheon of angels could do the same. That might be a valid criticism, but it is attacking the end of Kant's argument and doesn't address the issue of whether Kant is right to suggest that the universe is rational and that the summum bonum has to be in place within such a moral framework.

# Underground Map

The London Underground map can be used to help structure an argument in two ways. If you look at a map, not only are individual railway lines marked on it, but there are zones which indicate different distances away from the centre of London. A possible exercise is for you to analyse an argument or the key issues within a topic by placing the **CORE TENETS** of a scholar's argument or the main areas of a topic right in the middle of the map, with the less crucial sections (or consequential sections) flowing out from the core elements. This would be particularly useful if you are asked to 'identify key areas', which was one of the questions used earlier in this guide.

For example, take Hume's critique of miracles (see Practice Example 13). In zone 1, you would place his definition of miracles. You would then move to zone 2 and think about his core critique which is the overwhelming evidence for the laws of nature not being broken and hence the need for the testimony of miracle to be of sufficient nature to overcome the testimony of the established laws. You could then proceed outwards into other zones with the other arguments he gives against the likelihood of miracles. In each of these zones you could put a response that someone such as Swinburne gives to Hume.

Another way you could use the underground map is to put arguments or scholars on the branch lines. You will see that there are several points at which stations share a junction, but then branch off in another direction. Imagine doing this with arguments for God's **OMNIPOTENCE** for example – where do scholars cross over, on what points do they agree? Where do they then go with the separate development of their arguments? Do these separate arguments eventually meet up together again? Think of Aquinas, Mill, CS Lewis, Plantinga, and Ward on this issue. Where would they be placed on the lines?

Questions concerning the Nature of God could be very fruitfully mapped out in this way, and some good analysis would be carried out in the process. As noted, these are developed kind of mind maps or the **RIPPLE EFFECT** method of revision, but utilising a map such as the London Underground creates a sense of direction and cross-over of ideas and arguments.

It's also sufficiently different to help it stand out for you in revision, as long as you don't start mentioning the Bakerloo, District and Central lines in your examination answers.

# Exposing Fallacies

## Logical fallacies

The following fallacies or mistakes in logic (things that don't follow) are found in any course of philosophy. We can link this to one of our initial objectives to establish the consistency or otherwise of a theory. When considering a philosophical argument, one way of attacking the argument is to expose the mistake or fallacy which underlies the process of reasoning (rather than the foundational assumptions discussed above). We can introduce our exposure with a suitable analytic word "however" or "alternatively".

## Restricting the options

If I say "the world is flat or square" I am being forced to choose between two things neither of which are true. Such fallacies are argued even by philosophers (euthyphro's dilemma and Hume's fork are two examples encountered in ethics).

One philosopher, Rosalind Hursthouse, expresses this fallacy thus:

> "In some theatres where David Mamet's Oleanna was perfomed, a noticeboard in the foyer invited those who had seen the play to answer the question, "Who is right? Her or Him?", and thousands of people signed up saying "Her" or "Him". How could they possibly fail to see that the alternatives presented…so signally fail to exhaust the

*possibilities? Neither was right." (On Virtue Ethics page 45).*

**EUTHYPHRO'S DILEMMA**, first expressed by Plato, sets up the following conundrum: is something good because God commands it or does God command it because it is good?  If goodness is good simply because God commands it, then it appears arbitrary what God commands - we cannot doubt or question God when he orders Joshua to slaughter the inhabitants of Jericho.

If God commands something because it is good then morality is independent of God and God becomes irrelevant to moral questions.

But notice here that there are only two choices. Suppose that a third view is actually the correct one: that God commands things because his character is good, and his character is the ultimate definition of goodness (love, kindness, compassion, mercy)? We are not allowed by Euthyphro's choice of two alternatives to argue for a third possibility: God's commands are good because his character is good. At essence it has nothing to do with what he says. If you want evidence of this, read Exodus 20 where a revelation of God's name and character preceeds the giving of the law.

## Slippery slope

Slippery slope arguments imply that if one thing changes, it will cause a slide into a disastrously bad situation. Of course this could be the case: for example, if we remove all traffic lights people will eventually ignore all traffic signals. But does it have  to be?

This possible fallacy exists particularly in the abortion and euthanasia debates. Free up the laws on euthanasia, it is argued, and there will be a general decline in human life.  But does this have to be true? Can't clear barriers be put in place to halt the slide or even prevent it ever starting? Is that what the new Starmer guidlines on euthanasia are trying to do: to clarify and define limits? Or the Oregon rules in America?

Exposing this kind of fallacy could for the core of any applied ethics essay. Notice that this isn't really a deficiency of logic, but an argument about probabilities.

## Analytic or synthetic: confusing the two

The statement "all swans are white" sounds like an analytic statement, true by definition. However the existence of black swans proves that it is actually synthetic, true or false by experience. By presenting it as a self-evident truth we cause people to disbelieve us when we present them with a black swan. In a sense, we close our minds to truth.

In the same way, if we say "God is good" by definition, we close our minds and can explain away the evidence in the world that God is not good (for example, random suffering and the sort of genocide that is described in the book of Joshua). If "God is good" is a synthetic statement, then we need to debate the evidence for or against, and sharpen up what we mean by "goodness". We might yet establish God is good, but we will do so on the basis of the evidence, rather than the fraudulent basis of defining him as such.

## Correlation does not mean causation

In the empirical world we observe things happening at the same time. Abortion rates rise as sexual morals change, for example. We might infer a causal connection between the two: a change in sexual morals causes a rise in abortion for example. But for this to be valid reasoning, we must establish that all other possible causes of the rise in abortions are not true. For example, poor contraceptive education or lack of availability of contraception or simply that people have access to abortion procedures who did not before. Causal links must be established, in every subject, not least applied ethics.

## Circular argument

We have already seen that the ontological argument for the existence of God may be an example of a circular argument. A circular argument begins in one place and ends up in exactly the same place.  If I say "goodness is what people desire, people desire happiness, therefore happiness is good", I have ended up exactly where I began, and we're arguably not much wiser about happiness or goodness. Yet this is exactly what Mill argues in his essay on utilitarianism:  "No reason can be given why the general happiness is desirable, except that each person, so far as he believes it to be attainable, desires his own happiness".

Another circular argument may be Aristotle's theory of natural law, adapted by Aquinas. This is based on the idea that goodness is something observable, defined by the ends or purposes rational people pursue.  But this argument appears to end up where it started: "the good is what most rational people pursue, rational people pursue money, therefore money must be good". This is discussed in more detail in the Natural Law handout on peped.org website.

# Generalising the particular (for example, Mill's proof of utilitarianism)

Bertrand Russell describes this fallacy thus: "This is the fallacy of thinking that because there is some property common to each of the individuals in the group, this property must apply to the group as a whole". Bertrand Russell (1872-1970[1]) gives an absurd example of this: it is true that every member of the human species has a mother, but it is a fallacy to say our species as a whole must have a mother. In the same way it is true that each one of us as individuals desires our own happiness, but it is a fallacy to say that 'the aggregate of individuals' desires happiness for the aggregate."[2]

Any question on meta-ethics could involve a discussion of the **NATURALISTIC FALLACY**. As the name suggests, this implies a mistake in reasoning. But what if the fallacy is itself a fallacy? For the implication is that we cannot validly move from an is statement "pleasure is good" to an ought statement "you ought to maximise pleasure". Yet this is exactly what many philosophical theories (such as utilitarianism and natural law) do. Are they all wrong to do so?

Here is a meta-ethics question which could employ a detailed analysis and evaluation of this fallacy, and maybe, as an A grade answer, expose the fallacy within the naturalistic fallacy. As with example 1 above, I have added my comments to show the strengths of the essay, in this different font.

---

1 Why I am not a Christian (1996) Routledge page 140

2 Jones et al (2006) page 74

# Practical Example 7

**"Moral statements are merely an expression of feeling" Discuss (OCR June 2011)**

*The branch of ethics that discusses the meaning and indeed the validity of the word good is called Meta-ethics, meaning 'beyond' ethics lies ethical language. From here there are two separate branches, cognitive; where "goodness" can be known as an analytic (Moore) or synthetic (naturalists like Mill). Philosophers divide between Naturalists who believe goodness is some observable as some property of the world and non-naturalists, and cognitive and non-cognitive; where "goodness" cannot be known as a property of the world. Within the non-cognitivists are another group called emotivists, they uphold the view that the word good is merely an expression of feeling. I partially agree with the emotivists view that moral statements are merely an expression of feeling, but I also think that as the 'good is so exceedingly ambiguous' (Stevenson) that any of the meta-ethical theories have validity to them.*

Excellent opening paragraph, demonstrating the crucial division and showing that you are taking a clear line on the question. I hope, though, that this student won't sit on the fence - not a good place to be in this debate.

*Emotivism says that moral statements merely express positive or negative feelings; it is mainly based on ...*

better to say "it's an empirical tradition which stems from..."

*...the work of the Scottish philosopher and empiricist Hume and the idea of Hume's fork. "When you pronounce any action or character to be vicious, you mean... you have a feeling or sentiment of blame." - David Hume.*

The student curiously doesn't tell me what the fork actually is - the analytic/synthetic distinction, but it's a very important point nonetheless.

*This idea was taken forward by A.J. Ayer who also believed that moral statements were primarily expressions of emotion, hence Emotivism, his theory has been called Hurrah-Boo theory.*

Why is it called this? Always give a brief explanation.

*An example of this is to imagine you and a friend are at a football game supporting different teams. When one team scores you cheer and your friend boos. According to this view, saying 'euthanasia is right' is the same as saying 'Hurrah for euthanasia!'*

This is a brilliant analogy because this is exactly what it means.

*This is the belief, called logical positivism, that any genuine truth claim must be able to be empirically tested and as moral judgements can't be tested they aren't genuine truth claims and therefore are only expressions of emotion. However, there are a few problems with Ayer's argument. Just because something is morally justifiable, such as abortion, doesn't mean that we passionately support its practice as he suggests in 'Hurrah-boo theory' as well as this, this argument is self-refuting. It claims that "Any genuine truth claim must be able to be tested by sense experience." But this claim itself can't be tested by sense experience. So, by its own standard, logical positivism can't be a genuine truth claim.*

This is a fascinating point and goes to the heart of the fallacy of composition Ayer and Hume make - it's an either/or fallacy eg "This table is either blue or red" closes off the options. Actually, the table is brown. See the chapter on fallacies.

*In contrast to the logical positivists and emotivists are duty based ethics, such as Kantian ethics. Kant believed that morality did not rest on sense experience as Hume would suggest but instead....*

moral maxims are derived (there's a missing phrase, which is why I've interrupted to supply it, so always read your work through)

*...through a priori reason, as ethical principles aren't empirical like an act utilitarian would state but instead are necessary truths for rational beings. Kant not only believed that emotion had no part to play in the meaning of the word 'good' but also in the way in which the 'good' was brought about. 'The good will shines like a jewel for its own sake.' - Kant. Kant believed that the absolute moral good derived from the categorical imperative had to be acted out purely out of 'duty for duties sake,' we should have no ulterior motive to do good other then it being the right thing to do, emotion contradicts with this virtue. Similarly, divine command theorists would state that what is good is what is commanded by God, and we should follow these laws out of our duty to God commands. I do not fully agree with the duty based ethics view on morality that it should be purely out of duty, I personally agree more with Hume's assumption that 'reason is the slave of the passions' and that the removal....*

the student means "addition", not "removal". Small mistakes do matter because they can suggest to an examiner a confusion and lack of clarity.

*...of an emotive force behind our morality makes it more virtuous then*

*purely 'duty for duty's sake.'*

The essay is crying out for a definition and discussion of naturalism here. One of the hardest things to grasp is that Kant who is normally described as a transcendental idealist (a non naturalist) is being redefined by some philosophers (such as Huw Price) as a naturalist who believes in the objective moral law - hard to grasp because it doesn't seem to fit with the idea of the a priori, but does fit with his phenomenal/ noumenal categories.

*However, another cognitive ethical perspective....*

At last we come back to the main point - I was getting nervous.

*....for a moment that contradicts both Kant and Emotivism is
Utilitarianism. On face value utilitarianism could seem quite similar to
Emotivism or logical positivism as what is morally good is what
provides the most pleasure to the greatest number, pleasure being an
emotion in most peoples opinions that is good. However, whereas in
Emotivism it is a matter of opinion such as 'hoorah for genocide' -
Hitler; for utilitarians the good is derived empirically as you can
measure the amount of people who would gain pleasure from an act
to those who receive pain. It is also for this reason that it contradicts
Kantian ethics as any teleological ethical theory does, as the rightness
or wrongness of an action are determined by its consequences rather
then the duty behind it...*

Technically the consequences linked to the one intrinsic good of pleasure or happiness.

*...but as well as this it's a selfish ethical theory where you act*

*hedonistically and the rights of the minorities can be neglected. However, arguably the good is still derived from feelings, but empirically rather then through opinion. On the other hand, many would argue that there is a difference between what is pleasurable and what is good, for example going out and getting drunk may be pleasurable but is it good?*

There's a nice little quote from Ayer to illustrate this point - see the handout on meta-ethics on the website referenced at the end of the book.

*If you can ask this question then goodness must be independent of the feeling of pleasure, this is Hume's and indeed Ayer's attack on naturalism and in this case Bentham's utilitarianism.*

*Another branch from meta-ethics is that of prescriptivism. Like Emotivism it is non-cognitive and it agrees that when we make a moral statement we are just expressing our own attitude, but Hare (the founder of prescriptivism) thought that we were also saying that we think other people "ought" to do a the same thing in a similar situation. 'This action can be universalisable and so I agree with it and you ought to as well.' - Hare. Prescriptivism shows how we can be both free and rational in forming our moral beliefs. Moral beliefs can be free because they express our desires and aren't provable from facts. They can be rational because the logic of "ought" leads to a method of moral reasoning that engages our rational powers to their limits. In this sense, it is very similar to the golden rule, 'do as you would be done by.'*

Yes, what the textbook calls the intrinsic sense of the word good, namely, that it is universalisable.

*This rule is a very rational one to follow in ethical thinking as it is relativistic so can cope with special situations unlike absolutist theories such as Kant and his 'crazy axeman'. But it also means that good is more than just an expression of feeling but an "ought" people should obey in similar situations, in this sense I think that it is a healthy progression from the perhaps idealistic yet unrealistic Kantian ethics.*

*In conclusion, out of the theories discussed and the ones that I have studied I find prescriptivism most appealing despite the fact that it says that ought judgments are universalisable imperatives, and not truth claims, this leads it to deny the possibility of objective moral knowledge and moral truths which seems to conflict with how we approach ethics in our daily lives. However, unlike emotivism it shows that the word good is more then just an expression of feeling but instead the basis of ethical rules, which gives it more weight as an argument. As well as this, as an ethical theory...*

Doesn't the student mean "as a theory of ethical language that gives space for principles and rules to be rationally debated" ?

*...where the rules are derived a posteriori there is a more relativistic scope then in Kantian ethics and divine command theory where their absolute rules can lead to immoral outcomes.*

Yes. If you look at the extract written by Hare on the site you will see he was trying to counteract the conclusion that emotivism came to that we cannot have rational moral debate, and Hare is successful in establishing that moral language is language of a certain type, admittedly neither analytic nor descriptive, but meaningful nonetheless. See Louis Pojman's textbook for a brilliant couple of pages on prescriptivism and moral principles.

This is an excellent A* answer because of its clarity, frequent glimpses of real insight, and its well-structured argument (plenty of technical language, names, quotes)..It doesn't quite get full marks for two reasons:

1. The paragraphs on Kant seem to deviate off the moral language point. They didn't need to. The student needed a clear description and definition of naturalism and here an evaluation of the naturalistic fallacy would have been very useful. Most philosophers are naturalists (Mill, Bentham, MacIntyre) at least the ones we study, and naturalism is a very defensible view - make the defence stronger in your analysis. Kant either isn't (traditionally) or is (modern reinterpretations eg Huw Price) a naturalist depending how you argue the case. It is now the emotivists who have gone into retreat.

1. The final paragraph is a little bit weak, I think, especially the last couple of sentences don't do justice to the quality of the preceding writing - a pity, because this student almost nailed this question.

Overall it scored in the exam, 32/35, Grade A*

# Evaluating Arguments

What is the relationship between analysis and evaluation? At the start of this book I criticised AS level for prising the two skills apart in the old specifications (and some of the new). This is because proper evaluation does both - it analyses and it evaluates all in one breath.

Consider the venn diagram below.

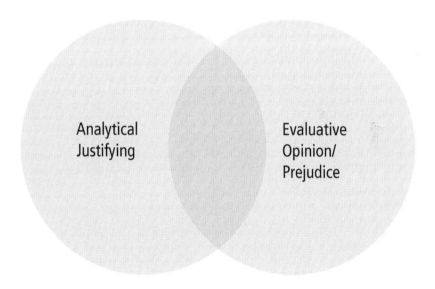

Analytical
Justifying

Evaluative
Opinion/
Prejudice

Let's start on the right hand side. There is a form of evaluation we do all the time as human beings - unreflective, opinionated judgements that border on prejudices. Consider the following:

- "I hate Manchester United'.

- "You're wrong!'

- "That's a stupid argument!'

- "I disagree totally with what you're saying'.

These are evaluations because they make a value-judgement (with words like strong, weak, right, wrong, hate, like). But they are not analytical value-judgements which we need to learn to make as philosophers. Here are some which we could place in the overlapping part of the venn diagram, because they justify the judgement (evaluation) we make. These are both analytical and evaluative.

- "Utilitarianism ethics is weak because it assumes we can easily calculate pleasure or happiness - but in practise we can't because I cannot easily ascribe hedons or other units of happiness to an experience".

- "Plato was correct: there is some ideal form of goodness that exists outside of our experience - it is set up by the way the world is made (a non-Platonic point)".

- "Dawkins asserts there is no purpose to creation but, paradoxically, he also says that human beings and other animals are driven by a survival urge. Surely this is a form of a purpose?"

Notice, turning now to the left-hand side of the venn, that it is possible to be analytical without evaluating, I do this by fully justifying, with reasons, why I am presenting an argument. I can also analyse by unpacking the structure of the argument itself (a slightly different point I considered earlier in the book). I do this by learning to disentangle the assumption-logic-conclusion which underpins the structure of any argument - which is rewarding as an exercise, and which I partly do in a table of assumptions and a discussion of logical fallacies (mistakes) you will find in an earlier chapter. Surprisingly enough, even philosophers make logical mistakes.

Finally there is a completely different way we can evaluate. We can ask 'is this true to the nature of the world and of human beings as I understand them?'.

Every philosopher, including you and me, is a child of their times. We are back with the importance of understanding the worldview within which we (and philosophers) write. Sometimes there is a paradigm shift (as Thomas Kuhn described it) in the way humans think - Galilleo was placed under house arrest in 1633 for suggesting the earth goes round the sun, and we too may be experiencing paradigm shifts in our culture. For example, the way women are viewed and, we hope, treated, is so different from the nineteenth century that we might describe this a paradigm shift. Women were considered in Victorian times to be too emotional to vote, too weak to play football and too unreliable to hold property when married. The old patriarchal view has died - but there again, patriarchal metaphors do seem to live on (such as Almighty Father as a metaphor for God).

To evaluate then is to be self-critical as well as philosophically critical of arguments. It is to look at the structure of arguments and the application of ideas.

So evaluation of the various arguments put forward in the essay is very often what differentiates a very good from a good essay. This key skill enables you to move from simply stating what the arguments are in your essay to what you actually think of them. One possible way to start your evaluation is to bring to the examiner's attention the arguments from scholars that have been raised against ones you have outlined.

For example, how does Dawkins argue against the design that Paley suggests is in the world, or, to use Dawkins again, how does his hard materialism act as an evaluation against Christian claims for post-death existence? This is evaluation of an argument using a **COUNTER-ARGUMENT**, and is best used where a scholar makes a direct critique of an argument put forward. Many textbooks are laid out purposefully to encourage you to see how a particular argument works, but also how it has been attacked. But we need to be careful here: make sure you use counter-arguments to show that you are evaluating the original argument; don't just put forward the counter-argument because you know you are supposed to.

## Building up Evaluation

We need to understand that philosophical writing does not make assertions that are simply left as they stand. Everything we argue needs to be justified, and justification requires a special type of language.

At the back of tis book you will find a list of analytical words and phrases. As an exercise, try highlighting such phrases and words in your next essay. What you find as an empirical fact   that C grade students have relatively few, and A* students naturally use many of these. One of my students, who scored 100% in every philosophy exam she did, had a favourite word - 'furthermore' - which is a good word, as it implies "I am going to push this argument just that bit further".

As we learn to evaluate we add evaluative language. Firstly there is a language that supports a point in an argument.  Here is a list:

- Logical

- Central

- Persuasive

- Strong

- Powerful

- Compelling

All these words suggest we approve a point - we commend it. Of course we haven't said why we support it - that is the analytical justification we need to add on.

We can also criticise a point by using words like:

- Illogical

- Tangential

- Questionable

- Weak

- Feeble

- Unconvincing

Notice I have taken opposites to the first list - and by looking up these words in a thesaurus you can add some more of your own. But remember we need to argue the case by saying "this is weak, because". Evaluation needs to be justified otherwise it is simply assertion, and that gains no credit. Once you have your first strength or weakness (evaluative foundations) you can then build upon each point, bringing in a name, concept or idea that supports or criticises this point. This can be achieved through using words and phrases such as:

- Furthermore

- X supports this view

- Defending this view

- This is reinforced by

Above all we must never simply state evaluation - many C grade answers develop into a list "Dawkins argues that there is no purpose to life on earth whereas Aquinas argues for a purpose". That is a contrast but not a very analytical one.

Much better to argue:

*"Dawkins' implies there is no purpose to creation but this appears to be an assumption because the inference that there is no purpose cannot be observed from creation itself - it is a metaphysical idea. The inference there is no purpose, paradoxically, is just as much a metaphysical idea as Aquinas' inference that there is. Moreover, Dawkins contradicts himself when he goes on to say there is a survival gene - an altruistic gene with a purpose to survive".*

# Critical Comparison

Many B or C grade essays have a sense of flow and purpose; the student knows the key components of the scholars' arguments and they have provided some responses to those positions by using, often successfully, counter arguments. The student then concludes by giving some fairly nondescript judgement. Such essays are on the podium and often in the right area but it sometimes surprises the student that they fail to be awarded an A grade.

I would argue that there has been a lack of critical comparison of the strengths and weaknesses of the arguments and the counter-arguments that have been put forward in the essay. Putting forward arguments and counter-arguments alone is not enough. Evaluation of those arguments is needed, and one way that can be carried out is by building on what you have done in evaluation by stating your **PHILOSOPHICAL JUDGEMENT** as to why the strengths of Dawkins outweigh the strengths of Paley or vice versa.

Why do you think that an argument carries greater philosophical merit? Have you uncovered a missing **PREMISE** in one of the arguments? Do you think that a position takes a leap in logic and therefore does not work, and because, you suggest, it does not work it cannot be philosophically justified – what about Copleston's contention that 'everything within the universe is contingent therefore the universe itself is contingent?' Does this work?

Or, for example, do you think James has successfully established the reality of a religious experience, despite the possibility that some of those experiences may have been illusory, as Freud suggests? In revision, we need to think about what we will argue and what arguments we are more philosophically convinced by.

If you have been brave in your opening paragraph, you may have indicated the line that you are going to argue, (the **THESIS**), but in that opening you did not state why you were going to pursue this line. Critically weigh the arguments up; you have seen how they act against one another and the way they evaluate the **STRENGTHS** and **WEAKNESSES** when they are placed against each other (and, as I say, any good textbook will help you with how the arguments look against each other in evaluation). Now you assess how they critically compare with each other under your own philosophical lens (using the personal pronoun "I" if you so wish).

So many essays are ones in which the voice of the student is never heard. What are you going to argue? Don't miss out this crucial stage. It does not really matter where you do it in the essay, but it would seem logical that, after you have seen how the arguments act as evaluations against each other, you add your own robust evaluation through critical comparison of the merits of the arguments you have used in your essay.

# Assessing Essays

## AO1 and AO2 criteria

In 1999 The Religious Studies Subject Criteria defined 'what candidates know, understand and can do' in terms of two Assessment Objectives, (**AO1 & AO2**).

*At A level, candidates are required to demonstrate their knowledge and understanding, and their ability to sustain a critical line of argument in greater depth and over a wider range of content than at AS level.*

*Knowledge, understanding and skills are closely linked. Specifications should require that candidates demonstrate the following assessment objectives in the context of the content and skills prescribed.*

*AO1: Select and demonstrate clearly relevant knowledge and understanding through the use of evidence, examples and correct language and terminology appropriate to the course of study.*

*AO2: Sustain a critical line of argument and justify a point of view. (OCR Assessment Criteria)*

The difference is sometimes expressed in this way: at AO1 level we are expected to analyse and describe with **KNOWLEDGE** and **UNDERSTANDING** the key. At AO2 we are being asked to judge and evaluate with **JUSTIFICATION** and **CRITICISM** being the key. Put another way - AO1 asks us to string together a line of argument with full reasons, clear illustrations and citation of relevant philosophers (even with short quotes to illustrate what they say). AO1 writing will typically use connector words like **because** (justifying with reasons) **in order to** (spelling out the consequence and purpose), **moreover** (implying something more to say) and **furthermore** (implying you will push the point a bit further).

AO2 writing will be analysing assumptions, and their validity, evaluating arguments as strong or weak and pointing out fallacies (mistakes in an argument) and other flaws (such as the inability to apply an idea in practice.) AO2 writing will typically use connector words like **however, on the other hand**, in **contrast, against this view, but**, and **nonetheless**.

# Indicative Content

Indicative content is a summary of the sort of content that might be expected as an answer to a question. But it is not the only content possible, just as there may be several ways of answering a question and intepreting the intention of the assessor.

Here is a question from a 2015 A2 exam paper:

# Practical Example 9

## To what extent can it be believed that religious experiences are no more than illusions? (OCR, G981, 2015)

The trigger phrase 'to what extent' invites a response that is qualified - for example, 'to some extent' may mean 'in so far as the experience cannot be verified empirically it must be taken to be subjective' (for example). But it may also invite a response which says either 'they are wholly illusions' or 'they are not illusions at all'. The main thing is to be clear before you launch the essay what your basic approach (what I have called your **THESIS**) is going to be.

Next, we need to discuss and consider the key ambiguous term 'illusion'. It is ambiguous because it has more than one meaning. An illusion can mean a 'trick' as in 'optical illusion'. A person says they've seen a ghost or met with Christ on the road to Damascus (St Paul). Is the mind playing tricks on the religious person?

Or illusion can mean something like 'your experience may be valid but the interpretation is not". This lies behind Hobbes' view that a person who says God spoke to him in a dream is only saying that he dreamed God spoke to him. The 'illusion' here is not that the person has seen a ghost and their mind has played tricks, or thought they heard a voice, but that they took a common experience of dreaming and turned that by an interpretation into the objective-sounding phrase - "God spoke to me in a dream'. Much the same thing can happen with the experience of healing - someone gets better (objective fact - unarguable) becomes 'God healed me' - which could well be an illusion. So we need to understand the nature of the illusion before we can analyse its validity.

Here is the OCR exam board's description of indicative content for this question. Notice the use of tentative words like 'may' and better responses are 'likely' to mention.

*AO1 Candidates may begin by exploring the notion of human beings believing that they are capable of having direct knowledge of God; part of the problem with this idea is that since God is so different from human beings, what would count as a direct experience of God? It is therefore natural for others to believe that the person having the experience is delusional. They may use Hobbes' view that a man who says God spoke to him in a dream is really just saying that he dreamed God spoke to him.*

*Better responses are likely to focus on some rather than all types of religious experiences lest they fall into the danger of simply writing a list They could, for example, simply analyse the statement in terms of conversion and corporate experiences.*

*Some candidates are likely to use William James as part of their AO1 material but they should avoid simply explaining 'passive', 'ineffable', 'noetic' and 'transient' and not applying them to the question as many have done in the past.*

*Those who are arguing that these experiences are not illusion may describe the writings of thinkers such as St. Paul, Teresa of Avila or Julian of Norwich. Others taking an opposing view may look at scholars such as Christopher Hitchens or Richard Dawkins.*

*AO2 Those who wish to assess the idea that there is more to a religious experience than illusion may explore the notion that evidence can be found in the changes often found in the way those who have experienced God in some form or other live their lives. The obvious one to choose would be St Paul, but there are many others whom candidates may have studied.*

*Alternatively, some may argue that no matter how big the change in a person's views, an alleged experience could still be an illusion which just happily made someone a better person from some other person's perspective.*

*Others may argue that people only have experiences which fit into the religion in which they have been brought up. So, for example, Christians do not 'see' or 'hear' Ganesh or Kali but rather 'see' the Virgin Mary or weeping statues. The best responses are likely to integrate their evaluation into their explanation of the issues.*

# Levels of response

Any essay can only be marked accurately if the marker has the levels of response in front of them. These give, in broad sweeping statements, an overview of the way an essay is banded by certain criteria which are met excellently, very well, well, moderately well or rather poorly.

Consider the **AO1** levels of response for OCR marking at A2 level. In this board there are six at A2 and five at AS. Other boards have only five at each. The intention is the same - to identify quickly the band the essay falls into.

**AO1** Demonstrates knowledge and understanding of religion and belief

## Level 6 (14-16 marks)

An **excellent** demonstration of knowledge and understanding in response to the question:

- fully comprehends the demands of, and focusses on, the question throughout

- excellent selection of relevant material which is skilfully used

- accurate and highly detailed knowledge which demonstrates deep understanding through a complex and nuanced approach to the material used

- thorough, accurate and precise use of technical terms and vocabulary in context

- extensive range of scholarly views, academic approaches, and/or sources of wisdom and authority are used to demonstrate knowledge and understanding

## Level 5 (11-13 marks)

A **very good** demonstration of knowledge and understanding in response to the question:

- focuses on the precise question throughout

- very good selection of relevant material which is used appropriately

- accurate, and detailed knowledge which demonstrates very good understanding through either the breadth or depth of material used

- accurate and appropriate use of technical terms and subject vocabulary.

- a very good range of scholarly views, academic approaches, and/or sources of wisdom and authority are used to demonstrate knowledge and understanding

**Level 4 (8-10)**

A **good** demonstration of knowledge and understanding in response to the question:

- addresses the question well

- good selection of relevant material, used appropriately on the whole

- mostly accurate knowledge which demonstrates good understanding of the material used, which should have reasonable amounts of depth or breadth

- mostly accurate and appropriate use of technical terms and subject vocabulary.

- a good range of scholarly views, academic approaches, and/or sources of wisdom and authority are used to demonstrate knowledge and understanding

## Level 3 (5-7)

A **satisfactory** demonstration of knowledge and understanding in response to the question:

- generally addresses the question

- mostly sound selection of mostly relevant material

- some accurate knowledge which demonstrates sound understanding through the material used, which might however be lacking in depth or breadth

- generally appropriate use of technical terms and subject vocabulary.

- a satisfactory range of scholarly views, academic approaches, and/or sources of wisdom and authority are used to demonstrate knowledge and understanding with only partial success

## Level 2 (3-4)

A **basic** demonstration of knowledge and understanding in response to the question:

- might address the general topic rather than the question directly

- limited selection of partially relevant material

- some accurate, but limited, knowledge which demonstrates partial understanding

- some accurate, but limited, use of technical terms and appropriate subject vocabulary.

- a limited range of scholarly views, academic approaches, and/or sources of wisdom and authority are used to demonstrate knowledge and understanding with little success

**Level 1 (1-2)**

A **weak** demonstration of knowledge and understanding in response to the question:

- almost completely ignores the question

- very little relevant material selected

- knowledge very limited, demonstrating little understanding

- very little use of technical terms or subject vocabulary.

- very little or no use of scholarly views, academic approaches and/ or sources of wisdom and authority to demonstrate knowledge and understanding

Let's try re-arranging them in a grid to try to make sense of them.

| Overall (mark) | Question | Relevant material | Know. & Underst. | Tech. vocab. | Scholars |
|---|---|---|---|---|---|
| **Level 6** Excellent (14-16) | Exclntly addressed | Excellent selection | Excellent | Wide ranging | Excellent range |
| **Level 5** V. Good (11-13) | Very well addressed | Very good selection | Very good | Accurate and approp. | Very good range |
| **Level 4** Good (8-10) | Well addressed | Good selection | Good | Mostly accurate and approp. | Good range |
| **Level 3** Satis. (5-7) | Generally does address | Mostly sound | Lacks breadth or depth | Generally approp. | Satis. |
| **Level 2** Basic (3-4) | General | Only partial | Some but limited | Some but limited | Limited |
| **Level 1** Weak (1-2) | Ignored | Little | Limited | Almost none | Little or no |

Notice there are five AO1 elements the marker is looking for: discussion of the question, relevance of selection, knowledge and understanding and technical vocabulary and scholarly views. You are being assessed on how well you blend these five elements together in your answer.

These are fairly generalised ideas but the advice normally given is to try to fix the broad band first. Is this essay best described as excellent, very good, good, satisfactory, basic or weak? It's worth imprinting these terms on our minds. Having decided which, we ask five questions:

1. How well is the question addressed? **QU**

2. How relevant is the material? **R**

3. How broad and in what depth is knowledge and understanding shown? **U**

4. How much appropriate technical vocabulary is there? **T**

5. How successfully and fully are scholars and philosophers mentioned and discussed? **S**

**QURUST** is I think a product that cures rust but how well it works as a mnemonic, I'm not so sure. You can now try the same analysis for AO2 criteria, worth a maximum of 24 marks at A2 - 60% of the total. You can find the criteria on the exam board website - my advice is to print it out and stick it on your notice board. If you're a marker, always mark with these AO1 and AO2 criteria in front of you.

# Missing the Mark

Sometimes students are mystified by the mark and grade they receive in August. A lot of time and money can be wasted on appeal because the student hasn't been coached to write to the correct level and so the grade cannot change. It is easy for even the brightest student to miss the mark, and in order to illustrate this, I am going to analyse in detail two answers which were written under exam conditions and explain why one only achieved D grade, and one failed to get an A* when it had started so well. As before, I add my own comments as I go along.

## Practical Example 9

### "To what extent is ethical language meaningful?"

Here is a C/D grade answer from a bright student

*Nineteenth Century ethics has been highly dominated by linguistics. Ethicists now work to discover the meanings of terms such as "good" or "bad". This goes beyond Normative ethics such as Utilitarianism, Kantian ethics or Virtue ethics but rather looks at the usefulness and meaningfulness of ethical language, known as Meta-ethics. It also tries to understand the meaning of terms used in descriptive ethics usually used by sociologists.*

This kind of generalised preamble is a waste of time. It confuses trying to sound clever with being a critical philosopher.

*Ethical language can be divided into cognitive language which is realist and objective, drawing ethical statements from nature and believing it to be true fact. On the other hand it can be non-cognitive, ethical language which is anti-realist and subjective. Logical Positivists, Ethical Naturalists and intuitionists believe ethical statements are true as they have a distinct purpose when using a particular word. Ethical Naturalists and Logical Positivists believe only Cognitive ethical language is true as it describes facts. Whereas descriptivists and prescriptivists argue although when referring to ethical language it may be subjective it still has significance and is of meaning. In this essay I will assess to what extent ethical language is meaningful, arguing it is fair to state all ethical language offers some instruction to society and is therefore meaningful.*

The thesis statement (the final sentence) should have been in the opening paragraph or even the opening sentence. In golfing terms, the student has spent a long time wobbling on the tee, introduced a lot of technical terms, but failed to get going.

*Ethical Naturalists argue ethical language can be understood by non-ethical, natural terms. Therefore the represent facts and can be proven to be true or false. For example, 'murder leads to the death of individuals' therefore murder is killing and ending a life and can be seen to be wrong. In this sense Ethical Naturalists would argue ethical language is meaningful as it can be proven and justified by real life empirical evidence.*

This paragraph is better because it discusses the question and makes a good solid point about ethical naturalism.

*Ethical Naturalists also argue ethical language has an underlined content of purpose. For example a knife is good if it cuts sharply. Therefore ethical language is showing what terms such as 'good' mean through the content of purpose within an ethical statement and is therefore meaningful in informing us on ethical terms such as 'good' or 'bad'. However, ethical Naturalists disregard the complexity of ethical language. This critique is put forward by G.E Moore, an intuitionist.*

This paragraph makes an assertion - about the 'content of purpose' in ethical language - and fails to ground the assertion by saying something like "through, for example, the link between goodness and maximising happiness, the purpose or telos of utilitarianism".

*Intuitionist G.E Moore. whose work is influence by David Hume. argues that it is wrong to derive an 'ought' from an 'is'. Although the world may be in a particular state it doesn't mean we can draw ethical terms from the natural word. Rather ethical language is sometimes used to discuss supernatural concepts such as God and therefore ethical naturalism's argument as to why ethical language is meaningful is absurd. Moore states we can still ask 'what is good?' this leads to an open question argument which displays the ethical naturalist argument as to why ethical language is meaningful may not be fully sufficient.*

An incoherent paragraph, unfortunately, because the connection between ideas is not made clear. Look at the sentence which ends with the word "absurd". This is just another assertion which makes no sense unless explained properly, and writing like this gains you no credit.

*However intuitionists do argue ethical language is meaningful but only due to the fact that intuition is used to conduct ethical*

*statements. Moore uses the Simple Notion to suggest although we
cannot fully describe what good is, we just know good is good and
that's the end of the fact. He uses the analogy of yellow, stating just
as we can't describe yellow without giving examples we can't
describe good without referring to good with examples. It is therefore
an indescribable truth. H.A Pritchard states ethical language is
meaningful as it is understood socially through intuition. W D Ross
goes further to state humans have innate sense of prima facie duties
discovered through intuition and when referring to ethical language
they again provide a social function in binding members to act in a
socially accepted way. However this disregards the fact that ethical
issues can be highly personal issues.*

This paragraph misses the point about the yellow analogy - that good is
irreducible further, says Moore - that yellow is just yellow and good is
just good. It also misses a central evaluative point, against Moore, that
'good' is like 'colour', not like yellow at all, because "good" is a general
catch-all term that includes many sub-terms within it, such as happiness,
desirability, duty, pleasure, a flourishing life (to name a few). It is
definitely reducible to other concepts. The style of writing this candidate
has adopted is neither analytical nor evaluative.

*On the other hand A J Ayer argues ethical language is merely
expressions of one's inclinations, emotions and feelings. He worked
closely with the Vienna Circle who brought about Logical Positivism.
Due to their belief that ethical language was simply expressions of
opinion they stated it is of little use. A J Ayer stated that there were
only two types of meaningful statements – analytical statements, ones
which contain the preposition with the statement e.g a bachelor is an
unmarried man, and synthetic statements, which are those that can be*

*tested by sense experience. Ethical statements do not fit into either of these categories and were therefore largely not meaningful to the Logical Positivists. Many may argue that this is a pessimistic and limited view of ethical language.*

The first half of the paragraph contains irrelevant assertions about the Vienna Circle: the second half is making an important and good point. But the point is not grounded in the conclusion that moral language simply expresses or 'evinces' (Ayer's word) a judgement or feeling.

*Despite A J Ayer's view that ethical language was simply of no significance and meaning due to it being subjective other scholars who take emotivism further such as CC Stevenson argue ethical language isn't only expressions of emotion but descriptively namely they derive from our perception and experience of the world and can therefore offer ethical knowledge to individuals. Ethical statements providing knowledge is of particular use especially when putting almost any ethical theory into practice as the majority can require a full sense of phronesis or practical reason or wisdom.*

The word 'subjective' is a dangerous one to introduce without explanation - Ayer didn't set the argument up like this. The rest of the paragraph is rather garbled and unclear - and then phronesis pops into the argument, but again in not a very helpful way. It's a word used by virtue ethicists taken from Aristotle, meaning 'practical wisdom' or 'prudence'.

*In addition Hare goes beyond descriptivism, stating ethical statements are actually prescriptive and therefore meaningful as they can act as imperatives. Not only are they saying 'boo' to murder or 'hurrah' to charity but stating 'I wouldn't steal, so neither should you' or 'I will give to charity so so should you'. In this sense ethical language is meaningful as not only does it provide universal norms or arouse feeling but place imperatives on what one sees as wrong or right, therefore offering some sense of guidelines to act ethically and morally. However one may argue why should one imperative be chosen over another?*

Much better paragraph, saying something interesting and basically correct about Hare's argument. But again, there is a lack of pattern and overall flow and logic to this essay.

*Furthermore the Swiss philosopher Piaget shows no language is meaningless as even babies respond by their own concepts. It is only until 11 years old that they acquire full understanding of all concepts. Nevertheless as long as concepts are not contradictory and make sense to those using them, like ethical language used in particular societies, it is not meaningless.*

I don't understand what this student means by 'even babies respond by their own concepts'. As a marker, it's not my job to interpret what you write. What concepts are we talking about here? What is a 'contradictory concept?"

*In conclusion one prime scholar who ultimately shows whether you believe ethical language is drawn from natural terms, intuitions or emotions, they all display ethical language which has meaning.*

*As Wittgenstein displayed in his 'dangerous game' all language is meaningful as long as the society using it understands the concepts. It is also clear to see ethical language plays an important social function in binding members of a society into a collective conscience and is therefore always meaningful.*

The conclusion is incoherent and doesn't follow from the preceding analysis. Wittgenstein is slipped in here and shouldn't be there as he hasn't been mentioned before. The main thesis hasn't been established that "in this essay I will assess to what extent ethical language is meaningful, arguing it is fair to state all ethical language offers some instruction to society and is therefore meaningful". How has emotivism, prescriptivism and intuitionism 'offered some instruction to society'? The essay would be awarded, at best, band 3, a low C grade or high D.

# Practical Example 10

## "Critically assess the view that free will and determinism are compatible"

This is an A grade essay that so easily could have been A*..

*To Sartre, the freedom of man to make choices leaves us all with a responsibility so great that we are 'condemned to be free'; Sartre is a libertarian who considers free will to lead to anxiety as to what we choose to do and become. Yet to Sam Harris, the challenge for man is to learn to accept that we live in a mechanistic universe ruled by cause and effect, which leaves no room for human freedom of choice; if we act based on our thoughts and emotions, and those things are determined by prior causes such as our upbringing and genetic make-up then our choices are predetermined and we cannot take one option over another at all. Can these two premises coexist within a coherent argument? This essay posits that free will and determinism, if defined in the normal sense of those words, are incompatible based on our current scientific understanding. Only the assumption of God's existence along with a particular theological stance, or future scientific discoveries, can lead us rationally to belief in free will; even then it will be in a very limited form. This writer subscribes to hard determinism but is open to the unlikely possibility of a limited form of freedom existing.*

Interesting thesis well expressed. Good rhetorical question half way down, a nice style of writing.

*Empirical evidence points towards hard determinism. Human behaviour is determined by the interactions of our genes with the environment around us. Within Anthropology this is not a contentious matter, so if choice is a form of behaviour it is safe to conclude that it is entirely determined. A Yale Professor of Social Psychology Stanley Milgram created an experiment to discover the extent to which humans are willing to torture or even kill another human being in order to follow instructions (respond to their environment). The experiment has been repeated, and has found that on average 75% of people continued to give electric shocks until the limit of 450 volts. Afterwards, when the experiment is explained to them, they are disturbed by what they have done, and cite reasons for their actions such as wanting to 'help research' and get the 'test right'. This goes to show the extent to which people obey authority unquestioningly, even if they are commanded to torture or kill, and is yet another example of humans responding to their environment. If we do have free will, it is in a limited form. However, the debate is not restricted to empiricism, and we shall assess attempts from other schools of thought to see if they can prove the existence of free will.*

Is it just genes? Or is this a form of scientific reductionism such as the statement 'the mind is like a computer". The mind does not have a screen like a computer - reality is constructed not just by brain waves but by what we believe. So what about beliefs, arguments and thought processes – metaphysical entities bound up with the mystery of perception? How do these affect choice? How do you act when you stop believing in free will? I would argue you behave very differently (for example, you may give up more easily). Therefore the case for hard determinism is rather overstated here and needs more evaluation.

*David Hume argues that not only are free will and determinism compatible, but that free will cannot exist without determinism. This is because freedom itself rests upon the assumption of determinism. When one chooses one thing over another, they do so because they know that if they choose X over Y, they will receive X rather than Y. That is to say that they expect the cause - their choice - to lead to an effect. This confirms their acceptance of a mechanistic universe. To defend free will, then, one must show that it is different from other aspects of the world which are determined and that the human will is uncaused. If something is uncaused then it is random, for if there was anything that prevented it from being random one would call that thing a cause. If our free will is based on randomly selected choices, then we are still not free, but rather subject to uncontrollable chance. This problem arises when we speak of free will as the opposite of determinism, when in fact indeterminism is its true opposite, and constraint is opposite of freedom. Hume argues that an uncaused will is not the same as freedom, but instead freedom is the absence of constraint. To Hume, a human is free when their will is caused by internal factors, such as their beliefs, and values. A human is not free when their actions are determined by external factors. Thus, according to Hume, free will and determinism are compatible.*

Excellent – this writer has done what textbooks fail to do and explain Hume clearly!

*In order to make free will compatible with determinism, Hume dilutes freedom into something unrecognisable - he defines it in such a way that it is not really freedom at all. Locke's analogy from his Essay on Human Understanding shows that voluntariness (internally determined actions) is not enough for an action to be called free. If a man was locked in a room and could not physically leave, he cannot be said to be free even if he wants to remain in the room and would choose to if he had the choice. This is because freedom requires the ability to do other than that which one actually does - freedom requires viable options. Hume rejects this notion, arguing that if a person was found guilty of a crime, which they were not externally forced to commit, it does not make sense to say they would not have done it if things had been different. That is the same as saying they would not have done it if they were a different person. This is because internal causes such as one's beliefs, values and opinions based on accumulated experiences are part of that person's identity, whereas external causes are distinct from their character. Hume's theory may seem practical and is successful in maintaining moral accountability with determinism, but it fails because the distinction between internal and external factors is meaningless. In a mechanistic universe, the internal factors themselves are determined by external ones, and thus still cease to be within our control. On a separate point, Hume rejects cause and effect when Aquinas uses it as a premise in his cosmological argument, but here he does not put his own premise under the same scrutiny. Kant was right when he referred to Hume's theory as a 'wretched subterfuge'.*

Another clear and rigorous paragraph. Good use a of a brief quote.

*Kant, paradoxically is both a compatibilist and an incompatibilist: within the phenomenal world there is no free will, but within the noumenal world where moral choices conveniently exist, there is free will. Kant attacked the notion of an uncaused will leading to random choices. He stated that the will exists in the noumenal world (a metaphysical world, quite Platonic in its nature) and is informed by practical reason, a metaphysical force which does not adhere to the cause and effect of the material world (phenomenal world). This avoids the problem of randomness, because the practical reason prevents choice selection from being down to chance, but Kant posits the existence of his noumenal world just as Plato argues for the existence of the Realm of the Forms, and it seems he does so because free will is necessary for the autonomy that must exist for his ethical theories to have value. Even if the noumenal world does exist, what causes a person to use their practical reason and thus freedom in the first place? Kant thought the process of thinking rationally involved eradicating emotion, which, if it were possible, would be an unnatural process and not part of innate human behaviour. Only some philosophers and readers of Kant would know how to access their free will, because only they would eradicate emotion and think rationally. Then one could ask what made those people read Kant's work initially? A friend gave them the book? That action exists within the phenomenal world and is therefore predetermined. Merely gaining access to practical reason and free will in the first place seems to be a predetermined process if we accept Kant's ideas. Although Kant has not successfully reconciled free will and determinism, he has highlighted that for the solution we may need to look beyond the empirical evidence and into the metaphysical.*

The paragraph starts with the word 'paradoxically'. A paradox s an apparent contradiction which can be discussed and unpacked. A* students use paradox as a weapon to elevate the quality of their arguments.

*Theism may be able to offer proof of free will, if one accepts God's existence and the divine nature of scripture. God commands man to act morally, which suggests we are capable of choosing between right and wrong - something which involves free will. Perhaps in Genesis when God made 'man in his own image', that signified our unique ability to exercise free will. A major problem for libertarians who are also Christians is that God is outside of time and omniscient, so therefore has foreknowledge of what his creation will go on to do. Calvinists hold that God must therefore create some people to be saved - 'the elect' - and others to be damned - 'the reprobate'. This view is a hard theological determinist position, and is one which is of course so harsh it challenges many Christians concept of a loving God. Those who subscribe to Arminianism avoid this problem to some extent, by stating that just because God has foreknowledge of people's fate, their freedom to choose is not restricted. The Arminians argue that God desires to save everybody, but allows people to exercise their free will and reject him if they choose. It is questionable as to whether it is reasonable to think foreknowledge and free will are compatible here, because creating something in the knowledge of its fate seems no different than determinism.*

The first half of the essay sustained the argument very well — but this second half is beginning to feel like a list where the student is ticking off one branch of philosophy (or philosopher) after another and the argument is beginning to disappear. Never place knowledge before argument - it only leads to a loss of quality. Selection of your knowledge is the key.

*Daniel Dennett holds that the claim 'free will is an illusion' is like saying 'money is an illusion'. There is some truth in the claim but the implications of that truth are not what they seem to be. Dennett holds that we are still free in a sense for two possible reasons. He examines consciousness and states that the decision making process involves the formulation of multiple possible futures. The irrelevant or insignificant possibilities are rejected and those leftover undergo a reasoning process to determine which one shall be selected. The second stage in which a possibility is selected is predetermined, according to Dennett, but the initial process of possibility generation could be uncaused. Dennett suspects that this process is caused, but because it is advantageous from an evolutionary perspective for the possibilities to be randomly generated, the causes will be things as insignificant as the position of the planets or what one had for breakfast. However, Dennett is open to the idea that quantum mechanisms in the brain could produce uncaused ideas. This avoids the intelligibility problem, whereby the rejection of determinism destroys the possibility of purposeful actions and thus choices, because the indeterminism is limited to this one area. However, as Dennett recognises himself, this random possibility generator inserts indeterminism in the most insignificant place, meaning that while the future is not predetermined, we are none the less not truly free.*

Interesting, but again the argument is becoming lost and there doesn't seem to be a clear conclusion rounding up the discussion. As ssona s your essay develops into a list it is starting to fall off A* grade.

General points:

1. This is a very bright student who writes very clearly with an excellent style. The good thing about the essay is the first half – he establishes a clear thesis and makes some very interesting points. However, he then weakens the essay by failing to stay on track – which means continuing to discuss the question paragraph by paragraph.

2. The essay would have been much better if he had crossed out the theism section and maintained the momentum of the first half discussing (essentially) the different meanings of 'cause' 'freedom' and 'the will'. The debate does actually hinge on these three meanings because philosophers disagree because they take different views of these three terms. For example. The hard determinists take a very mechanistic view of cause and effect – like the billiard balls. A libertarian disagrees: the metaphor of billiard balls itself is misleading. There is arguably such a thing as a metaphysical cause. They argue that a change in belief may occur, for example, after I convince you of a point. The 'cause' here, inserted in any chain, is in fact a mental debate between two people in which I change your belief system. And beliefs themselves are actually metaphysical.

3. So, if he had changed tactic half way and developed this very interesting point about causation, freedom and the will and its different meanings and then rejected the Humean and libertarian arguments for clear reasons, he would have been awarded full marks (yes, it's possible to get full marks). This involves tactically saying less, but arguing more and my final point...

4. He absolutely must have a conclusion. The conclusion restates the

thesis which he so excellently stated at the beginning and then adds nuances to that conclusion to clearly establish the case, in a summary form. This is now the skill he would need to focus on – state the thesis then establish the thesis selectively (don't try and say too much!) and then restate the thesis in a slightly more nuanced form as a conclusion. Do this and I can see no reason why this candidate shouldn't get close to full marks in the exam. Using the OCR exam descriptors of different levels which applied up to 2017 we have:

**AO1 Level 4 17/21** A good attempt to address the question, accurate knowledge, good understanding, good selection of material, technical terms mostly accurate. Communication: generally clear and organised

**AO2 Level 5 12/14** An excellent attempt which uses a range of evidence to sustain an argument, comprehends the demands of the question, shows understanding and critical analysis of different viewpoints. Communication: answer is well constructed and organised (I have given this level 5 rather than 4 - a risk falling off a level because of the points I've mentioned above – in other words, this could easily have been awarded 11/14 which would still give an A, just about).

Overall: A grade 29/35 (82%)

Note that from 2018 A2 essays will be marked out of 40 for OCR board, with AO1 allocated 40% of the mark (maximum 16) and AO2 60% (maximum 26).

# Making Up Your Own Questions

If you're going to learn how to write really good A level essays I suggest you start by making up your own exam questions. This may sound like a strange thing to argue in a book about essay-writing, but the more essays I read the more I'm convinced that students, and indeed some teachers, haven't really studied the specification and tried to understand the mind of the examiner.

Every year I play a little game - I pretend I'm the examiner and publish my paper on the peped website. One reason I do this is not to convince everyone I have a strange prophetic gift, but rather because I think many students are taken by surprise by some of the twists in exam questions. When you're sitting there nervously at your table writing for those words 'you may now start' is not the time to discover the mind of the examiner.

Consider the following example. In my predictions for 2016 A2 OCR paper I posted this question:

> "Natural law is the best approach to issues surrounding contraception". Discuss

I did this deliberately to remind students that moral theories studied the previous year at AS level can crop up again in the actual A2 question. This may surprise some. If you haven't studied Natural Law for a year it would be somewhat disconcerting to dredge your memory when you have just three minutes planning time on exam day.

The question that was actually asked wasn't quite this one.

*"Kantian ethics is the best approach to issues surrounding sexual ethics".*

You can see, however, that it was s similar type of question, taking an AS normative ethical theory and connecting it to an A2 applied issue.

So let's imagine we are the examiner setting an A2 paper for the new OCR Developments in Religious Thought (Christianity) paper. We have to observe the following rules.

1. No technical vocabulary can be named in the question that isn't in the specification.

2. Questions cannot cross over areas - each area of the syllabus has questions set just on that area.

3. Questions will have trigger words that have been decided beforehand (there can be no new trigger words). This list includes the following (for OCR): discuss, critically discuss, to what extent, assess, critically assess, evaluate, analyse, and critically compare. So every question we face will have one or other of these trigger words.

# Analyse the Specification

Now we need to open the specification (available online) at H573/03 Developments in Christian Thought. Like a detective we are looking for an insight into the examiner's mind. What do we find?

First of all there is a long introduction - one page, in which the examiner tells us 'learners will explore religious beliefs, values and teachings, their interconnections, how they developed historically and how they are presently discussed". From this I can deduce I need to do:

a. **Some Bible study**. Matthew 25:31-46 (the parable of the sheep and goats) is mentioned in the specification. In the section (2. Foundations) on the Person of Christ a number of passages are mentioned: on miracles and the Son of God title, Mark 6:47-52, John 9:1-41, on the idea of a 'teacher of wisdom', the Sermon on the Mount, Matthew 5:17-48 and Luke 15:1-11, and on 'Jesus the liberator', Mark 5:24-34 and Luke 10:25-37. But notice also there are quite number of suggested passages as well. You must study those listed as part of the syllabus, and you would be wise to pay attention to the second list of 'suggested passages' (and why not study some more that are relevant?

b. **Some history.** In the Knowledge of God section there is no explicit reference to anybody. But in the suggested scholarly views Calvin's Institutes are mentioned. In fact, read the OCR textbook and you will see Calvin's views get prominence, particularly the tension in Calvinism between natural and revealed theology. You need to be clear that you don't have to mention Calvin at all in your essay on knowledge of God. But as guidance, one thing you could do is look carefully at what Calvin says abut the issues of natural versus revealed knowledge and be prepared to quote him (or some other historical figures from the Reformation period).

c. **Some present day discussion**. Plantinga is a present day academic who writes about knowledge of God - you could discuss him. John Polkinghorne is another. The Catechism of the

Catholic Church is mentioned in a number of places in this specification as suggested reading (on Augustine, Death and the Afterlife and the Person of Christ). One way of studying for this paper is to contrast throughout the Catholic official teaching with a Protestant Church (the Church of England, the Baptist Church or the Lutheran Church for example). If you are an A* candidate you might also consider that no Church has one view on any doctrinal issue, and mention some of the tensions within the churches and their various wings.

d. **Some interconnections.** We are philosophers now, and pretty much any connection between the Bible, ideas, history and the present day is relevant. We can use this specification to become culture readers. Original sin lurks as an assumption still in our culture, for example, in Mrs Thatcher's address to the Presbyterian Church of Scotland in 1989, where she criticises the idea that human nature is 'perfectible' as a socialist myth. But you also see it in the media, which seems to lurk around every corner waiting for a celebrity to 'sin' and then be 'exposed'.

Notice also that there are tensions within the ideas themselves which you can explore in your essay. Calvin argues both that we are made in the image of God and that we are tarnished and spoiled by sin. So how much of the image of God remains? Arguably when a distinguished Leeds surgeon drowned trying to save two teenagers in difficulty off the coast of Cornwall in 2015, he died showing this image of God is very much alive - in the self-sacrifice and altruistic tendency present in our nature.

Then we find at A2 level three big ideas are introduced: pluralism, feminism and secularism, with the emphasis on how faith and reason interact and address issues around a multi-faith society and the fairly new stress on women's rights. Christianity now exists in a secular context, but you could say, it struggles to become visible. Will Christianity eventually disappear under the weight of secular challenges, both in intellectual attack by the likes of Dawkins and lifestyle attacks caused by things like the change in human sexual practices?

As I study the new specification I find myself getting excited. Remember that nothing is ruled in or out as long as it is relevant to the issues and the question set. So I suggest we become brave and adventurous - if we don't like John Calvin, for example, then we are welcome to find someone else who addresses the large issue of natural and revealed theology and the relationship between them.

# Set a question

What clues are there in the syllabus about what questions might be set? The answer is, 'many clues'. Although the official syllabus, that's the part that doesn't have the word 'suggested' in it, may be rather broad and general, the guidance given is quite specific. Let's illustrate this by looking at what the syllabus suggests about Augustine.

The examiner has invited us to consider 'issues related to Augustine's ides of human nature'. He is referring particularly to the idea of original sin, that we have fallen into a state of condemnation before God because of the first sin of Adam, as St Paul puts it 'as in Adam all die'.

We can turn these suggested issues into exam questions in the following way.

**Issue**: 'whether or not Augustine's teaching on the historical Fall and

Original Sin is wrong'.

**Exam question**: To what extent is Augustine's view of human nature an accurate account of the origins of sin in the Bible?

Now try changing the trigger word and see if the feel of the question changes. It's worth considering what difference the trigger word makes.

"Analyse and evaluate Augustine's account of the Fall of Man".

**Issue**: 'whether or not Augustine is right that sin means that humans can never be morally good'.

**Exam question**: Evaluate the view that original sin means human beings are incapable of moral behaviour.

**Issue**: 'whether or not there is a distinctive human nature'.

**Exam question**: "There is more than one natural human nature". Discuss with reference to Augustine's view of fallen mankind.

My argument here is simple. Take the specification and turn it into exam questions using the method outlined above. Practise interpreting trigger words like 'discuss' and 'to what extent'. Keep the clues ever before you as you study and very likely you will get an A grade. There are twenty-one ready made question 'starters' (issues, as above) in this section on Developments in Christian Thought, year 1, alone.

All we need is the discipline to use the clues provided and unlock the secrets of the examiner's mind.

# Self-diagnosis

Let's assume you are now genuinely trying to address the question in front of you and have understood the implications of the question and the importance of starting with a clear thesis or one line summary of your approach.

If we recall the examiner's AO1 criteria of assessment there were a number of elements to it.

- Use of technical vocabulary

- Breadth and depth of knowledge and understanding

- Relevance of material

- Scholars introduced and discussed

- And, one I'm going to add which crosses into AO2 criteria, evidence of analytical and evaluative writing

## 1. Technical vocabulary

A student may be using technical vocabulary but in the wrong way. Let me illustrate this with an example. Imagine I am writing an ethics essay on natural law. I decide that the following technical vocabulary is relevant (taking the mind-map introduced in an earlier chapter as my guide): teleological, synderesis, primary precepts, secondary precepts and eudaimonia.

The question before me reads: "Evaluate the natural law approach to determining right from wrong".

I begin my essay like this: "Natural law is a teleological theory which generates primary and secondary precepts from a synderesis principle in order that eudaimonia results". This is a weak opening because although the statement is correct, it doesn't display understanding. It is just a list of technical vocabulary.

Technical vocabulary should be used to demonstrate understanding. Compare this second attempt: "Natural Law theory it teleological because, in Aquinas' version, the end or true purpose of all rational beings is to fulfil the true intention of their creator and live lives that flourish. To do this, we need to pursue rational goals or primary precepts that are worked out by practical secondary precepts - either moral rules or social laws which build the ordered society. The issue here is - how clearly and practically can we discern these precepts and agree on the rules to follow?"

This is a much better attempt because the technical vocabulary is used selectively and woven together into an argument, which I conclude with a question (using the **AQUAQ** technique considered earlier.).

## 2. Evidence of analytical and evaluative writing

Analysis (AO1) and evaluation (AO2) is a certain style which can be measured by the use of analytical words and phrases. A full list is given at the back of this book, but let me here highlight a few of them.

• Develop a point by using words like furthermore and moreover, which add something new., or of spelling out the implications, 'this implies'.

- Explain a point by using words like because or a phrase like in order to.

- Contrast a point  or idea by using phrases like 'on the other hand' or 'in contrast'

- Illustrate a point by using phrases like 'for example' or 'for instance'.

- Say something interesting by using a word like 'paradoxically' which points to an implied contradiction. For example, 'paradoxically, Aquinas argues that we always intend to do the good even if we are mistaken and even Hitler sought to 'do good and avoid evil'.

- Be evaluative by using words like 'however' or 'but'.

I said that this is evidence of an attempt to write analytically and evaluatively. It is worth working in pairs with a friend and highlighting your use of such 'connectors' as these, that is words and phrases that connect the building blocks of your answer together and give them a sense of purpose and direction. But a word of warning. If you re-read the essay I marked on page 76 you will see that you can use connectors like 'however' and 'furthermore' in a weak and ineffective way.

# 3. Breadth and depth of knowledge and understanding

An examiner is looking for evidence that you know something about, say, natural law and that your knowledge is not superficial. So imagine in the essay given above that I am developing a point about the rather tricky word **SYNDERESIS**. I can either make a rather generalised assertion such as 'synderesis is Aquinas' starting point - that we 'do good and avoid evil'. Or I can make a deeper and broader point. I've put my comments in brackets.

> *"Synderesis is the first principle of the natural law, argues Aquinas, because synderesis is an innate quality, given by God, by which we know and recognise and desire the good goals of the fulfilled life (depth of knowledge). This will and conscience directs us towards our ends irrespective of whether we believe in God. It gives natural law its universal aspect - every human being, argues Aquinas, shares in the natural tendencies of our rational nature (breadth of knowledge - widening out the analysis to spell out implications).*

## 4. Relevance and use of scholars

In this essay below I have commented extensively on the use of scholars, their views and introduction of contrasting viewpoints. It's worth reading this example carefully and ask yourself - couldn't `I write like this? Notice also how analysis and evaluation are woven together. Evaluation should never be tacked on at the end as an afterthought.

# Practical Example 11

## Evaluate Hume's claim that miracles are the least likely of events.

*In his Essay on Human Understanding, David Hume argues in one chapter strongly against belief in miracles. This is primarily through an argument for credibility. As the sun rises every day, and we have never seen any different, although we cannot say with one hundred per cent certainty that it will rise tomorrow, yet it is shown by observation to be so likely as to eclipse reasonable doubt. If, therefore, says Hume, a man tells us that the sun stood still, as Joshua does in the Bible, we ought to weigh the probability of the sun having done as it always does, against that of lying, or being mistaken.*

This opening paragraph presents a very clear thesis in the form of an "If..then". This gives the student a direct way in to analysing the question: evaluate both sides of the If..then clause. Is the conditional plausible or not? Does the "then" really follow from the "If"?

*There is an argument advanced against this by Richard Swinburne, the principles of credulity and testimony. The first is that if a man thinks he saw something, there is more reason than not to believe he saw it, and second, there is more reason than not to think that when a man gives testimony of something, he is telling the truth.*

Straightaway, we have a counter-argument and contrasting view from Richard Swinburne. A dialogue is being established between two views.

*However, this is very weak compared to the astonishing claims made for miracles, such as that previously mentioned; and Hume would argue that it is more likely a man should be drunk, or diseased, or mistaken, or lying, when he makes such a claim as that the sun ever stood still, than that he truly saw it, as weighed with our constant observation.*

The writer's view is clearly expressed : he finds Swinburne's view weak, for the above reasons. Notice the technique here: thesis, counter-thesis, writer's conclusion (after evaluation). Evaluation is woven in.

*Another argument advanced by Hume is that no miracle has ever been witnessed, or verified, by a large body of men of upstanding character, good intellect, and lacking in credulity. This is certainly true, though one may argue in turn that few things ever have.*

The essay plan is unfolding. We have David Hume view 1, now we have David Hume view 2. You can almost see the essay plan in front of the writer. Knowledge and understanding are being carefully revealed with excellent selection of material.

*Another is that miracles have only tended to appear in what he calls savage, uncivilised nations or times. The founding period of ancient civilisations, he notes, is filled with heroes and monsters and astonishing miracles; but always, when education and use of letters became widespread, these stories diminish and disappear, whether in Rome, Greece or England - for example, Homer's Iliad, and King Arthur's tales. This argument is generally true and universally sound, though there have been miracles observed in civilised nations also, such as appearances of the Virgin Mary and even the hard-hearted Samuel Johnson thought he had seen the ghost of his friend, Edmund Cave.*

The third argument in the plan is presented and immediately evaluated.

*Yet another is the multiplicity of miracles; for so many religions and nations claim their own, that it is impossible to believe all could be right, when so many even contradict, as, for example the Bible and the Qur'an upon Jesus' divinity. There are so many, that they must necessarily cancel out, and in the process show miracles to be an inaccurate superstition of human nature. While individual religions may answer that only their miracles are correct, and all others wrong, this only serves to bolster Hume's point; ten thousand claims to infallibility cannot be correct.*

And a final supporting argument to the main thesis that Hume's criticism of miracles is sound. A good use of illustrative example here, of the Bible and the Qur'an which present a very different picture of Jesus - that of prophet in the Qur'an and eschatological Lord in the New Testament.

*In sum, all Hume's arguments are for credulity, or what is overwhelmingly the most likely to be true; against what is not. And upon evaluation, they are very sound. Every principle of common life is formed upon that basis. One does not expect one's house to be in Herefordshire one day, and Shanghai the next; nor should one, because the overwhelming sum of observation shows that houses do not move, nor does the sun stand still.*

*It is undoubtedly true that, while theoretically possible, no-one would deny a miracle seen at first hand, though perhaps even then it would be more logical to attribute it to madness - that such an event as a miracle could occur, for as Polkinghorne and Swinburne say, scientific laws are really mere observations of what we see happen, not what must happen, or cannot be suspended by a higher power, is possible.*

*But this is undoubtedly right to say that a miracle having occurred is the least likely event. Far more likely is, as he says, that reality should continue precisely as we observe it, than that someone's testimony upon the matter of, say, the sun standing still, can be trusted.*

A final precise, logical comparison between the sun and your house grounds this essay in a powerful evaluation. Unfortunately the final paragraph does produce one incoherent sentence in the middle of it, which reads as a self-contradiction to the main thesis (underlined). But for this momentary lapse, the essay would have scored full marks. As it is it gains a creditable 33/35 A*.

## Practical Example 12

Let's look at one more example - a full mark answer on Philosophy of Religion which truly exemplifies some of the principles we have discussed in this book, and gives a standard to emulate.

**'Critically assess the traditional Christian concept of God being eternal.' – OCR, June 2012, Q3 (Grade A)**

*The word 'eternal' has been defined in numerous different ways by*

*theist, agnostic and atheist philosophers. One such definition is that*
*for an object or being to be eternal, it must have a beginning but*
*never end (unless time itself also ends) – an object such as this exists*
*within time and will continue to exist until time itself no longer exists.*
*However, this definition is largely regarded as 'ever-lasting' as*
*opposed to eternal. Another definition of eternal then, is an object*
*which, although existing within time, has no beginning or end. This*
*definition is similar to the previous with one vital difference: the*
*object does not have a moment of conception; its existence is*
*inextricably linked to time and, for as long as time exists, so too will*
*this object exist (yet the object still does exist within time). The final*
*definition, however, contradicts both of the previous definitions and*
*states that, in order for an object or being to be eternal, it must exist*
*entirely outside of time. This is the definition upon which Christianity*
*traditionally places its belief of God as eternal and, as a result of this*
*fact, will be the definition discussed in this essay.*

An excellent introduction focuses on different definitions of eternal.
Everlastingness and timelessness as ideas lead neatly into a discussion of
Boethius, ensuring relevance and high quality.

*This definition of eternity in relation to God was put forward by*
*Boethius in his Consolation of Philosophy (524) and, since shortly*
*after the books' creation, has been regarded as the traditional view of*
*God's existence in relation to time; indeed, Aquinas supported this*
*view in his Summa Theologica, thereby further cementing it in the*
*Christian tradition. The view was initially put forward by Boethius as*
*an attempt to explain how humans could retain their free-will with an*
*omniscient God who could see every human's future: he reached the*
*conclusion that God must not exist within the time-frame which all of*

*humanity does.*

Notice how the two philosophers, Boethius and Augustine are placed in contrast to each other which implies excellent selection of material and use of scholars. The writing is subtle and concise - no superfluous detail is added.

*While God may know of our future, it is not the future for him as he does not exist within time. In this definition, God has no concept of time and exists in a continuous present with no concept of future or past; he sees all of human history in a simultaneous instant. Boethius himself explains this by stating that God has the 'simultaneous and perfect possession of boundless life.' While this theory may be strong and explained eloquently by Boethius, it has come under severe criticism by innumerable philosophers (particularly in the last century), both religious and atheistic including Richard Swinburne, Kenny and Brian Davies.*

Note that the candidate has correctly presented Boethius' contribution, though in 'Consolations of Philosophy' it is Lady Philosophy who reveals it to Boethius. When answering a question where you are required to distinguish between Boethius' dilemma, human freewill and rewards/punishments, and the solution to the dilemma, God's eternity, be clear about which voice you are detailing from 'Consolations': Boethius' or Lady Philosophy's.

*This being said, the traditional Christian view of God's eternity has a number of great strengths. Perhaps the greatest strength of the theory is put forward by St. Thomas Aquinas. He claims that, in the human world, change and time are blatantly inextricably linked: humans grow old and die, buildings erode and collapse, metal rusts and memories are forgotten. If God were to exist within time and be constrained by the same laws which time inflicts upon the universe, he too would be susceptible to change.*

God's attributes are now linked together for example, eternity and immutability (unchangeability).

*However, both the bible and Christian tradition state that God is ineffable and cannot change (in Malachi 3:6 it states that 'I the Lord do not change.'). Indeed, the ability to or even the possibility to undergo change seems to imply imperfection; a perfect being would have no need to change seeing as any change would be detrimental. Surely a God who ages, forgets or deteriorates in any way would not be worthy of worship. Clearly then, owing to the fact that God is perfect and the fact that he doesn't change, he must not exist within time.*

Use of quotations, such as the one fro Malachi, give a scholarly feel to the answer. Even if you can't remember the exact words, a paraphrase will do. Attributing the correct verse is a luxury few candidates manage - don't worry if you can't do it.

*However, despite the strength of this point, it has come under criticism, namely by Christian philosophers who believe that God is in fact capable of change. In the bible, God is shown to forge a covenant with the Israelites; he speaks of his love for them (as well as all mankind), asks them to perform tasks and gave them the Ten Commandments. Clearly, as is evident from human experience, it is impossible to take part in a relationship of any kind without it altering your way of life at least to a minute degree. Surely then, if God did indeed enter into a covenant with the Israelites, it must have altered him at least in some way, particularly if he loved them as is stated in the bible? Moreover, God is frequently referred to as having human-like emotions towards the people with which he creates relationships including surprise (Isaiah 5). Surely if God can be surprised, he is susceptible to change and, as a result of this the traditional view that God must exist outside of time owing to the fact that he cannot change may be fundamentally flawed.*

Here both sides of the argument are balanced up using analytical language - note the use of 'however', 'despite', 'moreover' and one rhetorical question in the middle of the paragraph. Superb. Evaluation is strong.

*Moreover, not only does God's ineffable nature cause problems with the traditional view of God's eternity when examples of relationships between God and humans are brought into question, but the very fact that God is able to form these relationships in the first place seems to contradict the traditional Christian view of God's eternal nature. Indeed, if Boethius' theory is to be accepted as the traditional Christian view, it seems to contradict any instances where God enters the human time-frame to intervene directly, whether that be through the answering of prayers, miracles or the coming of Jesus.*

Excellent linkage by way of illustration using the problem of miracles.

*According to the traditional view of God's eternity, he has no concept of past, present, future or universal time in general. Instead, Boethius and Aquinas would argue, he exists outside of time and sees all of humanities actions throughout all of time in a simultaneous, instantaneous present. If this were the case, it would surely be impossible for God to pick a particular time in history and intervene directly because God has no concept of human time. For example, according to Christianity, God directly intervened in the life of Mary and made her pregnant with Jesus, his son. This intervention from God on a specific date in history would arguably be impossible for a God who has absolutely no concept of time.*

A knowledge and understanding point: this is perhaps a slight misunderstanding of the notion of timelessness. It is not that God has 'no notion of time' it is more that 'God is not subject to time'. Boethius' presentation of God's eternity is one where God sees all of time laid out before him, like the many slides of a movie. In this way, one could theorise, God could do exactly what the candidate has dismissed; He could pick a slide and jump in, like Mary Poppins jumps into the chalk drawing.

*This criticism, therefore, has a very damaging implication. If the traditional view of God's eternity is kept then it would be impossible for any events throughout history where God directly intervened to be true (including the coming of Jesus). Owing to the fact that the vast majority of Christians would disagree with this statement, it seems likely that the traditional view of God's eternal nature demanding he be outside of time would be regarded as incorrect by most.*

The candidate has reasoned this point, albeit with some errors, which shows an attempt at justification. It is a good attempt to evaluate the involvement of God in the world, but perhaps the use of Wiles would be better to show that God could not be involved in the world as it would challenge his overall benevolence given that he picks and chooses where and when to be involved, e.g. in ancient Egypt and not in Auschwitz.

*That being said, however, it is possible for a Christian believer to retain his/her belief in the traditional view of God's eternity while still believing in direct intervention from God owing to a very simple explanation. While it may seem to be an impossibility for God to exist outside of time and manage to affect events within time, it is entirely possible that human's merely lack the mental capacity to fully understand God's nature and the way in which he acts. As an omnipotent being, it may be entirely possible for God to exist outside of time yet still will events to happen within our human universe. Indeed, Aquinas' theory of Eternal Law states that God's nature is only knowable through simplistic reflections and that the true complexity and power of God's true nature cannot be comprehended by us as humans.*

A lovely evaluation of human feebleness. The candidate could have drawn upon Boethius once more with the theory of knowledge and how knowledge of an object is relative to the subjective nature of the knower of the object.

*However, this is not a particularly strong point because, as Aquinas and C.S. Lewis state, and as is generally accepted by Christians, although God is all-powerful, he can still not perform actions which are logically impossible. Descartes disagreed with this and stated that God could do anything, whether logically possible or not. It would seem to many that being able to exist both within and outside of time is a logical impossibility and, as a result, cannot be done even by God. Therefore, I would argue that this point further weakens the traditional view of God's eternal nature.*

The candidate has used multiple scholarly opinions to evaluate this point about what is logically possible for God to do. It would be worth considering Descartes' position a little further. Descartes said that God can do the logically possible and impossible; typical responses would err towards Aquinas' notion that God cannot do what is logically impossible; this would defend God from challenges such as can God create a stone he cannot lift etc.

*However, upon reflection, Descartes' point holds some value: our understanding of logic and mathematics work insofar as we understand them and God wills them to work. Taking from Keith Ward, if we can know the universe it is because God has known it into existence; therefore what we know is what God allows us to know. Theoretically, therefore, what we consider logical is what God has allowed us to know to be logical. God could therefore have known into being what we consider illogical, thus Descartes is right. Ultimately, God created logic, so He can do what he wants.*

*A further, similar weakness of the traditional view of God's eternity is put forward by both Richard Swinburne and Anthony Kenny (both of whom are Christians). This weakness is similar to the previous as it is also concerned with the impossibility of acts which are logically impossible to achieve. Both philosophers argued that Boethius' idea of God seeing and knowing everything from outside of time in a simultaneous present is incoherent. Kenny attempts to highlight the ridiculousness of this theory by stating that, according to this view of God's eternal nature, 'The great fire of Rome is simultaneous with the whole of eternity.' Swinburne further supported this point and practically dismissed the entire theory by claiming that it 'doesn't make much sense.'*

Swinburne could have been discussed a little more clearly: he argues that God cannot know what it is like to be in 1995 unless He was in fact in 1995, which implies God must be 'in time'.

*It should be noted that both Swinburne and Kenny seem to be leaning towards a belief in God as ever-lasting as opposed to eternal in a Boethian sense. However, this criticism is extremely weak. Neither Boethius nor Aquinas claimed that all of time takes place at once; indeed, if this was the case it would be incorrect. Boethius instead claimed that the nature of God's knowledge is so different to humans' that he, as an omniscient being, sees all of eternity in a simultaneous present. The nature of knowledge which God possesses isn't constricted by time and, as a result of this, God is able to take in all the knowledge of the universe simultaneously; the events do not actually happen simultaneously. Indeed, Paul Helm puts this criticism succinctly and claims that 'God, considered as timeless, cannot have temporal relations with any of his creation. He is timeless in the sense of being time free.' He then goes on to accuse Kenny and Swinburne of reduction ad absurdum (over-simplifying the argument to ridiculous degrees to try and prove it as incorrect). For this reason, I would argue that Kenny and Swinburne's criticism doesn't weaken the traditional theory of God's eternal nature at all.*

Again, high quality writing here - with strong evaluation and quotation using Paul Helm.

*However, many have argued that Boethius' entire theory of God's eternal nature relies too heavily on the influence of Platonic and Aristotelian philosophy and isn't actually based in Christian knowledge. Indeed, the idea of a God who exists in a separate reality* from humans seems to be a Christianised reflection of Aristotle's idea of a Prime Mover God and his perfect, ineffability seems to draw from Plato's idea of the perfect, unchanging realm of the forms. However, I would argue that this criticism is extremely weak. Just because Boethius adapted some of his ideas from the ancient Greek philosophers doesn't mean that his theory isn't applicable to the Christian faith. Indeed, the mere fact that St. Thomas Aquinas supported the theory combined with the fact that it has been accepted as the general, traditional view of God's eternity seems to prove that, despite its roots in Pagan philosophy, it is entirely applicable to Christianity. Certainly, Christianity as a faith itself is largely based on ancient Greek Philosophy. For this reason, the traditional Christian view on the eternal nature of God is not weakened by its Platonic and Aristotelian roots.

Overall, therefore, I believe it is clear that Boethius' theory of the eternity of God as is put forward in his Consolation of Philosophy, which has been agreed with by Thomas Aquinas and generally accepted as the traditional Christian view is a strong, well thought out theory. However, despite this, I believe that this theory's apparent inability to support the view that God can interact with the universe, affect people directly and intervene at specific points in time weaken it significantly. Clearly, a huge percentage of Christians believe that God has the ability to affect what happens in our universe and, if the traditional view is to be accepted, it seems unlikely that this could be true. Therefore, I would argue that the fact that the traditional view of God's eternal nature seems to disagree with the traditional view of God's actions within the universe cause the theory to be far from perfect.

Perhaps we might have wanted a stronger conclusion which even examined a trinitarian standpoint - that the Father is eternal, the Spirit everlastingly present and the Son present in history and time. But overall this is an excellent full mark answer, constructed very well and ranging widely across a variety of philosophical views and eras. The challenges, for example, of Descartes and Swinburne are discussed and evaluated and the paragraph structure follows a pattern of examining different views of 'eternity' in turn. Finally engagement with the question is of the highest order: note how the candidate links repeatedly back to the question. At both AO1 level and AO2 this answer would gain full marks.

# Practical Example 13 - 16 Opening Paragraphs

It's very important to practise opening paragraphs, but at AS a different technique is needed: you must launch straight into your analysis. In order to illustrate the assessment criterion of 'addressing the question', notice how I go straight to the point in these examples, which are all from the Old OCR A2 Ethics syllabus. I also try to clarify all terms as early as I can.

## The weaknesses of virtue ethics outweigh its strengths. Discuss.

*Virtue ethics is the ethics of character and the formation of character through the exercise of phronesis or practical wisdom – a skill whose exercise builds right judgement in different situations. Proponents of virtue theory from Aristotle to MacIntyre argue that good character precedes right action. The central criticism of this theory, that it fails to guide action, is disputed by virtue theorists such as Rosalind Hursthouse, and the argument of this essay is that the central criticism is a misunderstanding, so the strengths do outweigh the weaknesses, and therefore the above proposition is false.*

## Assess the usefulness of religious ethics as an ethical approach to business.

*Christian ethics takes a number of different forms. In this essay I will apply three of these to the issues raised by business, particularly responsibility for the environment, for third world suppliers and for employees. The three approaches include a form of Christian relativism, as proposed by Joseph Fletcher, Situation Ethics; the deontological absolutism of Divine Command Theory and the unofficial moral viewpoint of the Catholic Church represented by Natural Law as originating in Aristotelean ethics and developed by Aquinas. What is distinctive about these ethical approaches to business, and how useful are they in practice?*

## Critically assess the claim that people are free to make moral decisions.

*Freedom, which is a much cherished belief of many, and a key assumption of Kantian ethics and Aquinas' natural law theory, may be an illusion. That is the startling claim of a hard determinist like Ted Honderich, tracing a long history that includes, for example, Thomas Hobbes. However, we do not have to accept the verdict of the hard determinist or the implication that moral responsibility is an empty concept and punishment should solely be for the protection of others. For any claim about free will (either for or against) is metaphysical, beyond proof. Moreover, we can take a third way between the extreme of Kant's metaphysics and Honderich's determinism, that of the compatibilist David Hume, who argues that for choice to make sense there must be an element of causal determinism, and so freedom requires determinism.*

## To what extent are ethical theories helpful when considering the issues surrounding homosexuality?

*In this essay I will contrast the view of psychologists such as Freud and behaviourists such as Skinner with the ethical theories of Natural Law and Situation ethics in order to try and assess which is the more useful approach, the ethical or the scientific. The issues surrounding homosexuality are three: the issue of origin of gender orientation, is it environmental or genetic, because if it's genetic then the idea of a "wrong" or "sinful" nature is surely refuted? Then there is the issue of conduct – cannot ethics give us general principles of conduct which could be applied to both homosexual and heterosexual behaviour? Finally I will examine certain assumptions we bring to this issue, for example, the assumption that there is one, universal human nature (which both Kant and Aquinas make). If we change the assumption, then does the ethical conclusion not change with it?*

# The Night Before the Exam

I have assumed throughout his book that you are an exam candidate, and so I want to write a chapter for you to read the night before the exam, which distills the advice we have been trying to demonstrate here.

Essentially there are two methods of writing essays on Philosophy, Ethics and Christian Thought.

**METHOD 1:** The thesis approach **TIDE**

In this approach, discussed in the second chapter, we state our thesis (conclusion) early in the first paragraph. We then develop the thesis in the body of the essay, illustrating it briefly and intelligently and presenting contrasting views if we so wish, (which we reject with good reasons). The thesis is then restated in a slightly fuller way (to reflect the careful analysis that precedes it) as a conclusion. **We should use this method when we are confident we understand the question and its implications**.

**METHOD 2**: The 'ask questions about the question' approach **AQUAQ**

Quite often we may not be very confident about what the question is driving at. If this is the case, then we must adopt the tactic of interrogating the question or asking questions about the question. I suggest we ask three questions and then spend a paragraph answering each one before coming to a conclusion. Each question focuses on one element of the exam question. **We should use this method when we are not fully confident about what the question involves.**

An example might help here. Suppose I have a question on ethics which asks:

*"The ethical issues around abortion cannot be resolved without first resolving the issue of personhood".*

What are the ethical issues surrounding abortion? How and with what ethical tools are these issues resolved? What is meant by the concept of personhood? These three questions (none of which have a single answer), woven into an opening paragraph, give the answer a clear, relevant structure - and the thesis should emerge as we develop our essay. The conclusion is then presented as our own answer to these three questions, perhaps arrived at by contrasting the views of specific philosophers and setting up two ethical theories to see how the idea of personhood is relevant to each.

An equivalent example in Philosophy might address the title "Religious Language is meaningless.", Discuss. The questions you might ask in your opening paragraph might include: What do we mean by religious language? Are there different rules for religious language when compared to everyday language? How is the word 'meaning' to be understood?

When you arrive in the exam room, you must follow the steps set out below.

## Read every question and highlight key words

Every year candidates make the fundamental error of learning a previous essay off by heart and then regurgitating it in the exam. And every year the examiner complains that candidates did not answer the question. So take a highlighter pen in with you and

1. Highlight all the **trigger/command** words (words like "explain", "to what extent", "discuss"). And then

2. Highlight any words that are **unusual** or unexpected.

If the trigger word is **explain** it is not asking us to **evaluate**. For example "explain the main principles of classical utilitarianism" has the unusual word "classical" in there. By focusing on this word and highlighting it, you are forced to ask the question "what is classical utilitarianism?" and so there is at least a chance that you will avoid the irrelevance of talking about Peter Singer, who is a modern utilitarian.

For Philosophy, sometimes a very specific question is asked to highlight an aspect of an argument, for example, 'Explain Descartes' ontological argument for the existence of God'. It won't gain marks if you go through other ontological arguments as this is not what the question is asking (you could highlight one or two differences, but only to stress the points that Descartes is making). Remember that when a scholar is mentioned in the syllabus, the question can be entirely addressed to that scholar - so the night before go through the syllabus check which scholars might come up.

But (just to be absolutely clear about this) at **A2 level** we are expected to interweave analysis and evaluation, and this is made clear by trigger words such as "discuss", "assess" or "to what extent".

# Sketch out your thesis/ key questions about the question

Always make sure there is some additional loose paper on your desk (put your hand up before the exam starts and request it). Then sketch out quickly your thesis, the main points you need to develop it, and any illustrations you may use. If you are genuinely unsure about the question, don't worry: every other candidate is probably unsure as well. Then use method 2 and ask three questions about the question and impose your own interpretation on it. You will gain credit by this considered and well-directed line which will then emerge as your answer.

My strong advice would be to practise sequencing ideas before the exam, and to have you own mind-map prepared and memorised which you can quickly sketch on a piece of paper as a memory aid.

# Be bold in your answer

It's surprising how many candidates come up with statements such as "there are many arguments for and against the ontological argument, and the issue remains difficult to resolve". This is a form of intellectual cowardice which gains no marks at all. Be bold in what you argue, and try hard to justify your approach with good, solid reasons. It is the quality of the argument which gains credit in philosophical writing, not the conclusion you arrive at. Of course, it essential that the conclusion follows.

# Analyse, don't just assert

It is tempting to throw down everything you know about, say, utilitarianism in a series of unconnected assertions.

> *"Utilitarianism is teleological, consequentialist and relativistic. It sets up the Greatest Happiness Principle. Utilitarians also believe the end justifies the means."*

These are just assertions which are peppered liberally with what we call technical language (that is language no-one in the real world ever uses). Notice that the above opening few lines demonstrate no understanding and no analytical ability. Instead we should be aiming to write more like this:

> *"Utilitarianism is a theory of rational desire which holds to one intrinsic good: pleasure or happiness. By the greatest happiness principle utilitarians seek to maximise this good in two ways: they seek to maximise net happiness (happiness minus misery) for the maximum number of people. So it is an aggregating theory, where goodness is added up from individual desires to produce an overall maximum good in which "everyone counts as one" (Bentham)."*

You should avoid phrases like 'this famous philosopher' and 'this issue has been debated for centuries'. Is this true? How would we know? Avoid these kinds of broad, sweeping generalisations.

# Illustrate your argument

I remember reading an exam report at University which mentioned that one candidate had been highly commended in an essay on utilitarianism for discussing the case of Captain Oates who, during Scott's doomed Antarctic expedition in 1912, walked out of the storm-bound tent in order to sacrifice himself to save his friends, with the words "I may be gone some considerable time". It's an interesting example because it suggests that a utilitarian could be capable of heroic sacrifice rather than the usual illustration candidates give of torturing a terror suspect to find a bomb location.

Spend a few moments working out which examples you will discuss to illustrate key theories and their application. You can pre-prepare them especially in Ethics, and in Philosophy of Religion you can pre-prepare the contrasting arguments which philosophers bring to many of the syllabus areas.

In Philosophy of Religion this advice applies especially to areas such as religious language and the analogies told by Flew (Wisdom's gardener), Hare (three blik illustrations) and Mitchell, (The Stranger), though be concise in how you illustrate these examples - always make them serve the point you are making and not the other way round.

# What is the examiner looking for?

In summary the examiner is looking for three things:

**Relevance** - every sentence linked to the question set and to your main thesis.

**Coherence** - every sentence and paragraph should "hang together' or cohere. The linkages should be clear as the analysis proceeds.

**Clarity** - your style should be clear, and in the context, the philosophical vocabulary you use should be clear. You don't necessarily have to define every technical word, but if it does need a little clarification, you can always use brackets for economy. For example:

"Utilitarianism is a teleological (end-focused) theory combining an idea of intrinsic goodness with a method of assessing that goodness by considering consequences".

An example in philosophy would be:

"The Falsification Principle argues that for any statement to be treated as a proposition it must deny at least one state of affairs rather than affirm all outcomes by expanding its criteria, (and in doing so, 'dying the death of a thousand qualifications', as Flew notes)."

# Analytical and Evaluative Words and Phrases

## 1. Producing reasons (justifying)

because
for this reason
this is supported by
this is justified by/ this argument is based on

## 2. Probing deeper (underlying)

this assumes
underlying this view
this worldview suggests
the implications are
this implies
from an X perspective

## 3. Adding something more (extending)

furthermore
finally
as a result
consequently
it follows that

moreover
also
therefore


## 4. Placing a counter-point (contrasting)

however
on the other hand
in contrast
this is directly opposed to
perhaps (with hesitation)
possibly (with hesitation)
maybe (with hesitation)
although
but
compared with


## 5. Concluding

in short
in conclusion
to sum up
I have argued
it has been established
the preceding analysis suggests

# Postscript

Peter Baron has a degree in Politics, Philosophy and Economics from Oxford University and a research degree in Theology from Newcastle. He qualified as teacher in 1982. He taught Ethics at Wells Cathedral School from 2006-2012, and in 2006 set up the community of schools which now numbers over 800 dedicated to sharing philosophy and ethics resources.

Today he is a freelance teacher and writer and author of several books on Philosophy and Ethics, including an AS and A2 Revision Guide for Ethics. He is a conference speaker with Academy Conferences, and every year offers a Revision Roadshow for students.

Other titles include - How to Get an A Grade, A Revision Guide to AS Ethics, A Revision Guide to A2 Ethics, Kant and Natural Law, Utilitarianism and Situation Ethics, Meta-ethics, Virtue Ethics, and Free Will and Determinism. These books are available in the peped shop, together with downloadable digital resources.

To join our philosophy community please register by going on our website, where you will find a wealth of material and further model essays: www.peped.org

16914077R00074

Printed in Great Britain
by Amazon